Annual Update

2012

GW00976060

US Government & Politics

Anthony J. Bennett

PHILIP ALLAN

Philip Allan Updates, an imprint of Hodder Education, an Hachette UK company, Market Place, Deddington, Oxfordshire OX15 0SE

Orders

Bookpoint Ltd, 130 Milton Park, Abingdon, Oxfordshire OX14 4SB
tel: 01235 827827
fax: 01235 400401
e-mail: education@bookpoint.co.uk

Lines are open 9.00 a.m.–5.00 p.m., Monday to Saturday, with a 24-hour message answering service. You can also order through the Philip Allan Updates website: www.philipallan.co.uk

© Anthony J. Bennett 2012

ISBN 978-1-4441-6889-1

First printed 2012
Impression number 5 4 3 2 1
Year 2016 2015 2014 2013 2012

Printed by the MPG Books Group

Hachette UK's policy is to use papers that are natural, renewable and recyclable products and made from wood grown in sustainable forests. The logging and manufacturing processes are expected to conform to the environmental regulations of the country of origin.

Contents

Chapter 1

Obama and the partisan presidency

The titles of a number of books on the US presidency contain three words: the definite article; an adjective and the word 'presidency'. There is, for example, *The Administrative Presidency*, *The Strategic Presidency*, *The Effective Presidency* and even *The Image-is-Everything Presidency*. Most famously of all there is Arthur Schlesinger's *The **Imperial** Presidency*. But how should we describe the US presidency today?

Political science professor Richard Skinner of Rollins College, Florida, has recently published a widely acclaimed paper in which he suggests that the 'modern presidency' — presidents from FDR to Jimmy Carter — has been superseded by the '**partisan presidency**' ('Barack Obama and the partisan presidency', a paper prepared for the annual meeting of the American Political Science Association, in Washington DC, September 2010). In this chapter we shall examine Skinner's thesis. We shall consider five factors which show the changes that have taken place from the era of the 'modern presidency' — presidents Franklin D. Roosevelt (1933–45) to Jimmy Carter (1977–81) — to the era of the 'partisan presidency' as characterised most clearly by presidents Ronald Reagan (1981–89), Bill Clinton (1993–2001), George W. Bush (2001–09) and Barack Obama. George H. W. Bush, whose presidency fell between that of Reagan and Clinton, operated much in the style of the 'modern presidency' and was therefore something of a throwback to an earlier period.

Relations with Congress

The modern presidency

For the five decades from the 1930s through to the 1970s, relations between the president and Congress were characterised by bipartisanship and cooperation. This was particularly noticeable when power in Washington was divided between the two parties — one party controlling the presidency, but the other party controlling both houses of Congress. This occurred during the Nixon and Ford presidencies (1969–77) when Republicans were in the White House but Democrats were in control on Capitol Hill. This is how Nixon's domestic affairs adviser John Ehrlichman saw relations between the Nixon White House and the Democrat-controlled Congress:

> [The President] was continually building coalitions in the Congress: on every issue that came up, a new coalition — a few southerners, some Republicans,

some interested Democrats who needed a judge approved in their District, or a bridge built, or a canal dug, or something of this kind — laborious step by step work, like putting together tiles in a great mosaic.

Notice how the Republican Nixon administration was building its ad hoc coalitions in Congress — they included 'interested Democrats'. Congressional liaison was bipartisan. It may have been time-consuming, but it was characterised by cross-party cooperation, what in Washington language was known as 'reaching across the aisle' — a reference to the central aisle in both the House and Senate chambers which separate Democrats sitting on one side and Republicans on the other.

In order to get legislation passed through Congress, it was necessary for both the White House and Congress to compromise. The noted British-American journalist Alistair Cooke once commented that American government was, at this time, 'based on three fundamental principles — compromise, compromise and compromise'. The president's legislative agenda was enacted by Congress only if it enjoyed cross-party support.

The partisan presidency

In contrast, the period of the partisan presidency has been characterised by little in the way of 'reaching across the aisle' and the absence of a willingness to compromise (Table 1.1). We saw this clearly in the negotiations regarding the raising of the federal government's debt ceiling during the summer of 2011. No longer is it a question of building ad hoc, bipartisan coalitions to pass the president's legislative programme. Presidents increasingly have come to rely on the overwhelming support of their own party in Congress and to expect the near-unanimous opposition of the other party. We have seen this during the Obama years with the passage of the economic stimulus package, the healthcare reforms and financial regulation. We saw it for George W. Bush over immigration and social security reform. We saw it for Bill Clinton over healthcare reform and the 1993 budget deal.

Table 1.1 Relations with Congress

Modern presidency	Partisan presidency
• Bipartisanship	• Partisanship
• Cooperation	• Lack of cooperation
• Cross-party coalitions	• Overwhelming support from own party
• 'Reaching across the aisle'	• Near-unanimous opposition from the other party
• Compromise	

Incoming presidents announce grand schemes to 'be a uniter, not a divider' (George W. Bush) or to 'end partisanship' (Obama). Obama did in the early months of his presidency seek to reach out to congressional Republicans, but to little effect. The same was true of George W. Bush's attempts to woo congressional Democrats. Admittedly the post-9/11 environment brought

Bush some bipartisan support but this was soon lost as a consequence of an unpopular war in Iraq.

The nature of political parties

The modern presidency

Throughout the period from FDR to Carter, political parties in the USA were rightly characterised as undisciplined, decentralised and ideologically diverse organisations. Each was 'a big, gaudy umbrella' under which people of different region and ideology could gather. Or to change the metaphor, they were 'broad churches' encompassing many different beliefs. They were largely state-based. The respective national committees were unimportant, the national committee chairmen pretty much anonymous, and the president played down his role as 'party leader'.

The 'modern president' such as Nixon or Carter showed little or no interest in fundraising or campaigning for candidates lower down the ticket in election year, and was hardly ever seen on the campaign trail during the mid-term elections. In the 1972 elections, while Nixon was winning 49 of the 50 states in the presidential race, his Republican candidates were losing hands down in the congressional races, winning a mere 192 seats in the House and only 42 seats in the Senate. In 1976, Democrat Jimmy Carter campaigned against the Democratic Party in Congress, running as a Washington outsider.

Neither did the 'modern president' seem to take much interest in the future of his party, though Nixon was a slight exception here with his 'southern strategy'. But presidents such as Eisenhower, Johnson and Carter showed little interest in trying to reshape the party during their term of office.

The partisan presidency

As we shall discuss in some detail in Chapter 4, the nature of political parties has undergone a significant change since the era of the modern presidency (Table 1.2). In the period from Reagan to Obama, political parties have become much more disciplined. The level of party cohesion we are now seeing in the US Congress is somewhat akin to what we've always associated with the UK House of Commons. Some American commentators are calling this the 'Europeanisation' of US politics. Parties in Congress are now looking and operating like parties in a parliamentary, rather than a presidential, system of government.

Table 1.2 Political parties

Modern presidency	Partisan presidency
Undisciplined	Disciplined
Decentralised	Centralised
Non-ideological	Ideologically cohesive
'Broad churches'	President as 'party leader'

Parties are now more highly centralised and nationalised, headquartered in Washington DC and, when the party controls the executive branch, in the Oval Office itself. National committees are more robust and national committee chairmen more visible and potentially powerful. We have even seen significant moves towards the nationalisation of congressional election campaigns, most clearly in 1994, 2006 and 2010.

Parties are now more ideologically cohesive than they used to be. No longer 'big gaudy umbrellas' or 'broad churches' but, as former Democrat senator Zell Miller once remarked, like 'upturned ice cream cones'. Furthermore, presidents of the partisan era have taken their role of party leader far more seriously. They campaign and fundraise voraciously for candidates further down the ticket in presidential election years and frequently travel thousands of miles to campaign for their party's candidates in the mid-terms. We saw both Clinton and George W. Bush try to reshape their parties' future ideological direction — Clinton trying to move the Democrats to the centre with his 'New Democrat' and 'triangulation' policies; Bush trying to move the Republicans more to the right with his neoconservative policies.

The nature and role of presidential advisers and bureaucrats

The modern presidency

Right from the days of the 1883 Pendleton Act and the establishment of a merit-based civil service, the phrase that was associated with federal bureaucrats and presidential advisers was 'neutral competence'. The phrase was widely used by presidents such as Teddy Roosevelt (1901–09), Woodrow Wilson (1913–21) and Dwight Eisenhower (1953–61). According to the Brownlow Report (1937) which led to the establishment of the Executive Office of the President, presidential advisers were to have 'a passion for anonymity'. Key White House staffers during this era were non-partisan experts, more interested in policy than politics.

The partisan presidency

But today, in the era of the partisan presidency, 'neutral competence' has been replaced with politics and spin (Table 1.3).

Table 1.3 Presidential advisers and bureaucrats

Modern presidency	Partisan presidency
• 'Neutral competence'	• Politicisation
• 'Passion for anonymity'	• In the limelight
• More policy than politics	• More politics than policy
• Non-partisan experts	• Spin doctors and ideological salesmen

The move towards a more politicised group of advisers and bureaucrats probably began back in the Nixon White House with folk such as Bob Haldeman and John Ehrlichman. At the start of his second term, Nixon devised a plan to form super-departments to bring the federal bureaucracy more under his political control. But the people and plans alike foundered in the Watergate scandal that would end Nixon's presidency in resignation halfway through his second term. However, Haldeman and Ehrlichman were merely the forerunners. President Clinton had Dick Morris and James Carville; President George W. Bush had Karl Rove. Even White House chiefs of staff became more political as the likes of Eisenhower's Sherman Adams gave way to folk such as Clinton's Leon Panetta and Obama's Rahm Emanuel. 'Neutral competence' has been replaced by spin doctors and ideological salesmen.

Relationship with the media

The modern presidency

Presidents of the FDR to Carter era used the media — increasingly that of television — to appeal over the heads of congressional and party leaders, directly to the people. To do this, they used what we might call the 'objective media' — not that there was much else during this era. By the 'objective media' we mean media that were objective in their reporting. Increasingly this meant the three terrestrial television channels — ABC, CBS and NBC.

The epitome of the objective media was Walter Cronkite, the anchorman of the *CBS Evening News* for 19 years, between 1962 and 1981. It was Cronkite who brought Americans the news of the assassination of President Kennedy on 22 November 1963, as well as reporting on the Vietnam War and Watergate, ending each broadcast with the line, 'And that's the way it is on...', followed by the date of the broadcast. Cronkite's increasingly sceptical reporting from Vietnam was thought by President Johnson to have been critical to public opinion. 'If I've lost Cronkite, I've lost middle America,' President Johnson is reported to have said. Known as 'Uncle Walter', he was once named by an opinion poll as 'the most trusted man in America'.

The partisan presidency

In today's era of the partisan presidency, presidents work not through the 'objective media' but what we might call the 'alternative media' (Table 1.4).

Table 1.4 Media

Modern presidency	Partisan presidency
Objective	Partisan
Trusted	Ideologically slanted
Ideologically neutral	New (or 'alternative') media
Non-partisan	
Old media	

The objective media — or what we sometimes call the 'old media' — were characterised by impartial, non-partisan political reporting. The alternative media — or what we sometimes call the 'new media' of cable television, the internet and radio talk shows — are characterised by partisan political reporting. A 2006 survey by the Pew Research Center found that 34% of Republicans regularly watched Fox News, while only 20% of Democrats did. One in ten Republicans regularly listened to Rush Limbaugh's radio show; only 1 in 100 Democrats did. Clinton spurned the objective media in favour of CNN and the internet, as did George W. Bush, favouring Fox News and conservative talk radio.

Obama has followed suit with liberal media outlets and bloggers, as well as liberal talk show hosts such as Ed Schultz. In his press conferences, Obama makes a point of frequently calling for a question from the representative of the liberal website *Huffington Post*, the African-American magazine *Ebony*, as well as the Spanish-language media.

Party approval gap

The modern presidency

Presidents in the era of the traditional 'modern' presidency won votes from across party lines and did not necessarily receive fulsome support from their own party's voters. Even in 1976, Democrat Jimmy Carter received the votes of only 80% of Democrat voters, with 20% of Democrats supporting Republican incumbent Gerald Ford. Four years later, President Carter received only 67% of Democrat votes.

Cross-party support was not only in evidence on election day, but also in opinion polls throughout the presidency. When pollsters asked about people's approval of the president's job performance, the gap between the approval rating given by those of the president's party compared with supporters of the other party was not that great. So, for example, as Table 1.5 shows, the average job approval rating of President Kennedy in his second year in office (1962–63) was 86% among Democrats but was still 49% among Republicans, thus giving an approval gap of just 37 points. The average approval gap for these six presidents during their second year of office was 35 percentage points.

Table 1.5 Gaps in presidential approval ratings by party during second year in office: Eisenhower to Carter [own party shown in bold]

President	Dates	Average second-year approval rating among		Party gap (% points)
		Republicans	Democrats	
Eisenhower	January 1954–55	**87%**	50%	37
Kennedy	January 1962–63	49%	**86%**	37
Johnson	November 1964–65	49%	**80%**	31
Nixon	January 1970–71	**82%**	41%	41
Ford	August 1975–76	**68%**	34%	34
Carter	January 1978–79	28%	**57%**	29

The partisan presidency

Presidents in the era of the partisan presidency win elections mainly by appealing to their own party's base, not by attracting voters from the other side. The change here seemed to come between the 1980 and 1984 presidential elections during the presidency of Ronald Reagan. It is this that leads us to claim that, just as FDR was the founding father of the modern presidency, so Ronald Reagan was the founding father of the partisan presidency (Table 1.6).

Table 1.6 Party approval gap

Modern presidency	Partisan presidency
• Attracts some cross-party support in elections	• Attracts negligible cross-party support in elections
• Some approval gap during presidency is evident	• Huge approval gap during presidency is evident

As Table 1.7 shows, the 1980 presidential election was the last election — discounting those with a significant third party candidate — in which the Republican candidate gained less than 90% of the Republican vote and the Democrat candidate gained less than 80% of the Democrat vote. It also shows how Reagan's partisan support had solidified between 1980 and 1984. In 1980, he received the votes of 86% of Republican voters, but by 1984 this had increased to 97%. Meanwhile, his support among Democrat voters fell by 10 percentage points from 26% to 16%. Even George H. W. Bush won the votes of 95% of Republican voters in 1988.

Table 1.7 Votes for presidential candidates by party, 1980–2008†

	Democrat voters		Republican voters	
Year	D	R	R	D
1980	69	26	86	8
1984	84	16	97	3
1988	88	10	95	5
2000	86	11	91	8
2004	89	11	93	6
2008	89	10	90	9

† 1992 and 1996 omitted because of Ross Perot's third party candidacy

Table 1.8 Gaps in presidential approval ratings by party during second year in office: Reagan to Obama [own party shown in bold]

President	Dates	Average approval rating among		Party gap (% points)
		Republicans	Democrats	
Ronald Reagan	January 1982–83	**79%**	23%	56
George H. W. Bush	January 1990–91	**85%**	53%	32
Bill Clinton	January 1994–95	19%	**73%**	54
George W. Bush	January 2002–03	**95%**	51%	44
Barack Obama	January 2010–11	13%	**81%**	68

Not only did cross-party support for the President fall on election day, but it also fell in terms of his job approval rating during his presidency, as is shown in Table 1.8. The average approval gap for these five presidents during their second year of office was 51 percentage points, compared with 35 percentage points for the presidents from Eisenhower to Carter. What is also clear from both Tables 1.7 and 1.8 is that these trends are more noticeable among Republicans than Democrats. But by the end of his second year in office, President Obama was the most polarising president of all with a 68-percentage point approval gap — exactly twice that of President Ford, even after Ford had controversially pardoned his disgraced predecessor Richard Nixon. Furthermore, as Table 1.9 shows, both of Obama's first 2 years rate in the top six largest approval gaps of all time, and Obama is the only president to feature in this table in his first 2 years. In this sense, President Obama is truly the partisan president.

Table 1.9 Largest gap in presidential approval ratings by party since 1953

President	Year	Date	Average approval rating among		Party gap (% points)
			R	D	
George W. Bush	4	2004	91%	15%	76
George W. Bush	5	2005	86%	14%	72
George W. Bush	6	2006	79%	9%	70
Barack Obama	2	2010	13%	81%	68
George W. Bush	7	2007	73%	7%	66
Barack Obama	1	2009	23%	88%	65
Bill Clinton	4	1996	24%	85%	61
George W. Bush	8	2008	67%	6%	61
Ronald Reagan	4	1984	89%	29%	60
George W. Bush	3	2003	92%	33%	59

www.gallup.com

Questions

1 To which eras do the terms 'the modern presidency' and 'the partisan presidency' refer?
2 Describe the relationship between the president and Congress during (a) the modern presidency and (b) the partisan presidency.
3 Explain John Ehrlichman's comment that 'building coalitions in the Congress [was]...like putting together tiles in a great mosaic'.
4 How did the nature of political parties differ during these two eras?
5 How did the nature and role of presidential advisers and bureaucrats differ during these two eras?
6 What did President Johnson (1963–69) mean when he said that 'If I've lost Cronkite, I've lost middle America'?
7 How has the president's relationship with the media changed?
8 Compare the data shown in Tables 1.5 and 1.8. What changes do they show?
9 What does Table 1.9 tell us about presidents George W. Bush and Barack Obama?

Chapter 2

President Obama's re-election prospects

What you need to know

- Presidential elections are held every 4 years.
- This is fixed by the Constitution.
- Federal law fixes the date as the Tuesday after the first Monday in November.
- The last presidential election was held on Tuesday 4 November 2008.
- The next presidential election will be held on Tuesday 6 November 2012.
- Since the passage of the 22nd Amendment (1951), presidents are limited to serving two terms in office.

The doyen of US political commentators Rhodes Cook had this to say in his *Crystal Ball* (www.centerforpolitics.org/crystalball) column in February 2011:

> When it comes to presidents and re-election, two things seem clear. If they appear to be in control of events, they win. If events seem to be controlling them, they lose.

Four months later, Republican strategist Karl Rove wrote an article in the *Wall Street Journal* ('Why Obama is likely to lose in 2012', 23 June 2011) explaining the reasons why he thought President Obama would probably lose his re-election bid in 2012. He came up with some quite convincing arguments: an economy that is proving stubborn to rejuvenate; a sharp decline in support for Obama among key groups of voters such as independents and seniors; foreign policy missteps and high gas prices. As Rhodes Cook further commented:

> Put all this baggage together and it would probably be enough to sink the Titanic, no iceberg needed.

Even so, forecasting the results of presidential elections, even ones in which an incumbent president is running for re-election, is a tricky business, especially as I'm writing this exactly 1 year before election day. Few would have thought at the close of 1991 that President George H. W. Bush would lose the following year's election to Governor Bill Clinton of Arkansas. But lose he did.

Come November 2012, will President Obama appear to be 'in control of events' or controlled by them? There are some trends to look out for, and in this chapter we shall consider four things that incumbent presidents need to do in the months running up to their re-election in order to enhance their chance of winning.

Avoid an intra-party challenge

Since 1960, there have been eight presidential elections in which the incumbent president has run for re-election (Table 2.1). Out of these eight elections, on five occasions the incumbent president won and on three occasions he lost. There is no discernible trend by party: Democrats have had two wins and one loss; Republicans three wins and two losses. But there is one variable which has in all these eight elections matched the result. Discover for each of these eight elections the answer to this question: did the incumbent president face a significant challenge from within his own party for the presidential nomination, or did he have a free run through the primaries to the nomination?

Table 2.1 Elections featuring an incumbent president running for re-election, 1964–2004

Year	President	Party	Result
1964	Lyndon Johnson	Democrat	Won
1972	Richard Nixon	Republican	Won
1976	Gerald Ford	Republican	Lost
1980	Jimmy Carter	Democrat	Lost
1984	Ronald Reagan	Republican	Won
1992	George H. W. Bush	Republican	Lost
1996	Bill Clinton	Democrat	Won
2004	George W. Bush	Republican	Won

As is shown in Table 2.2, five of the eight presidents — Johnson (1964), Nixon (1972), Reagan (1984), Clinton (1996) and George W. Bush (2004) — faced no significant intra-party opposition in the presidential primaries. They all went on to win a second term, three by a landslide. The remaining three of these eight presidents — Ford (1976), Carter (1980) and George H. W. Bush (1992) — *did* face significant intra-party opposition in the primaries and all lost their subsequent bids for re-election.

Table 2.2 Link between intra-party challenge to incumbent president and eventual result of election, 1964–2004

Year	President	Significant intra-party challenge?	Won/lost
1964	Lyndon Johnson	No	Won
1972	Richard Nixon	No	Won
1976	**Gerald Ford**	**Yes**	**Lost**
1980	**Jimmy Carter**	**Yes**	**Lost**
1984	Ronald Reagan	No	Won
1992	**George H. W. Bush**	**Yes**	**Lost**
1996	Bill Clinton	No	Won
2004	George W. Bush	No	Won

This is unlikely to be a mere coincidence. If an incumbent president receives a challenge from within his own party, it first says something about the insecurity of his political position in the country at large. Second, it means that by the time he meets his *general* election opponent, he is already damaged goods. In 1992, Bill Clinton was able to adopt some of the critical slogans which Republican Patrick Buchanan had used against President Bush in the primaries. Third, it also means that a great deal of his hard-raised money has to be spent in the primaries against fellow party opponents rather than being saved for later use against his *real* opponent.

In this respect, 2012 looks like good news for President Obama. There is no significant challenge going to be made to the President in the Democratic primaries. So in this way, 2012 will be another 1996 when another Democrat president — Bill Clinton — had a free run in the party's primaries, and then went on to win easily in the general election. But there are some dark clouds on the horizon for the President, ones that were not there in 1996 for President Clinton.

Avoid poor economic news

Bill Clinton had been elected in 1992 amid a serious economic recession presided over by his Republican predecessor George H. W. Bush. When Clinton arrived at the White House in January 1993, the US unemployment rate stood at **7.3%**, but that turned out to be its peak. Unemployment fell throughout Clinton's first term and by January 1996, the dawn of his re-election year, stood at just 5.6%, and would fall to **5.2%** by October, just before the election (Figure 2.1).

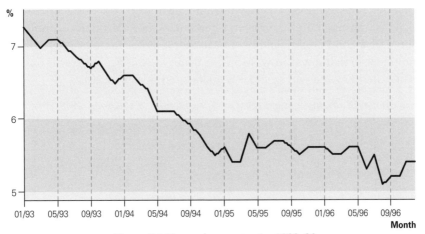

Figure 2.1 Unemployment rate, 1993–96

Source: **www.bls.gov**

Barack Obama finds himself in a very different position. When Obama arrived at the White House in January 2009, unemployment stood at **7.8%** — pretty much where it was at the start of the Clinton presidency. But the rate climbed inexorably throughout Obama's first year, peaking at **10.1%** in October 2009. It then started to decline, but nowhere near as steeply as during President Clinton's first term, remaining at **9%** in October 2011 (Figure 2.2).

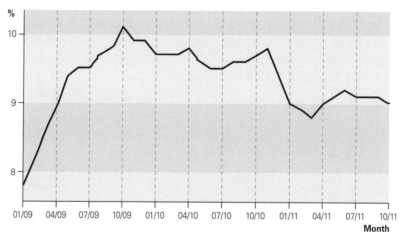

Figure 2.2 Unemployment rate, January 2009 to October 2011
Source: **www.bls.gov**

Table 2.3 looks back at the ten presidential re-election bids between 1948 (Harry Truman) and 2004 (George W. Bush). Only Ronald Reagan (1984) was re-elected with an unemployment rate above 7%. Ford (7.7% in 1976), Carter (7.5% in 1980) and George H. W. Bush (7.3% in 1992) all lost. True, Reagan was re-elected — in a landslide — with unemployment still at 7.4% in October 1984, but that was down from a peak of 10.8% at the end of 1982. Reagan was given credit for an over-3 percentage-point drop in unemployment within 2 years and could claim — in the words of his famous 1984 television commercial — that it was now 'Morning again in America'. It seems out of the question that Obama will be able to make such boasts in 2012.

Table 2.3 Unemployment rates and presidential re-elections, 1948–2004

Year	President	Unemployment rate in re-election year (%)		Won/lost re-election
		January	October	
1948	Harry Truman	3.4	3.7	Won
1956	Dwight Eisenhower	4.0	3.9	Won
1964	Lyndon Johnson	5.6	5.1	Won
1972	Richard Nixon	5.8	5.6	Won
1976	**Gerald Ford**	**7.9**	**7.7**	**Lost**
1980	**Jimmy Carter**	**6.3**	**7.5**	**Lost**
1984	Ronald Reagan	8.0	7.4	Won
1992	**George H. W. Bush**	**7.3**	**7.3**	**Lost**
1996	Bill Clinton	5.6	5.2	Won
2004	George W. Bush	5.7	5.5	Won

But, of course, the national unemployment statistic masks state-by-state differences. In August 2011, for example, unemployment nationally stood at 9.1% but this varied between 13.4% in Nevada and 3.5% in North Dakota. There are, however, some health warnings with regard to these state-by-state statistics. The state with the second highest unemployment rate in August 2011 was California, at 12.1%. No one is seriously suggesting that because of that, President Obama will lose the state of California. Neither is anyone suggesting that North Dakota voters will suddenly give the President a majority of their votes because their state's unemployment is so low. Where the state-wide unemployment rate may play a significant role is in those swing states with higher than average rates of unemployment. At the end of this chapter, we shall identify seven key battleground states. Of these seven, Nevada and Florida are the only two that currently have above average unemployment rates, making the President's job all the more difficult in these two states. We ought to add to those two the state of Michigan, a state which the President ought to win but at the time of writing has the third highest unemployment rate in the nation.

Table 2.4 Unemployment rates in selected states, August 2011

Five highest state-wide unemployment rates	Five lowest state-wide unemployment rates
1 Nevada: 13.4%	46 Oklahoma: 5.6%
2 California: 12.1%	47 New Hampshire: 5.3%
3 Michigan: 11.2%	48 South Dakota: 4.7%
4 South Carolina: 11.1%	49 Nebraska: 4.2%
5 Florida: 10.7%	50 North Dakota: 3.5%

Source: **www.centerforpolitics.org/crystalball**

Another economic indicator that seems to be important when considering a president's approval with voters is gasoline (petrol) prices. George W. Bush's approval rating reached rock bottom in mid-2008 as gas prices reached a record high of $4.05 a gallon in July of that year. The average price for a gallon of regular gas across the USA on the day Obama began his presidency was $1.81. By the end of October 2011 the average price had reached $3.48, slightly down on the peak of $3.90 it had reached earlier that year. That represented a doubling of gas prices for the average American. Republican politicians clearly think that high gas prices are something for which voters will punish Obama in November 2012, should this remain an issue.

The state of the US stock market as measured by the Dow Jones Industrial Average, however, is a much less clear guide to a president's re-election chances. When President Bill Clinton was beset by one of his many 'relationship' scandals during his first term, one of which concerned a certain Paula Jones, Americans were said to be 'more interested in Dow Jones than Paula Jones'. Be that as it may, or maybe not, there is very little correlation between the ups and downs of the Dow Jones index and presidential re-election. Both

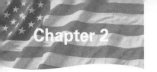

Richard Nixon and George W. Bush saw the value of the stock market fall overall during their first term, yet they were re-elected; Gerald Ford and George H. W. Bush both saw the stock market rise yet went down to defeat. On Obama's first day in the Oval Office the Dow Jones index closed at 7,949. By 3 November 2011, a year before election day, the market closed at 12,062. That's a larger percentage rise than even Reagan or Clinton saw during their first terms. But the President may not receive much credit for that if other economic indicators are still gloomy.

Avoid approval ratings below 50%

No president has been re-elected to office with approval ratings below 50% 1 year before election day. Indeed, as Table 2.5 shows, the only president to be defeated for re-election having had an approval rating of over 50% 1 year out was George H. W. Bush. His approval rating in November 1991 was 56%, but that was down from 66% 1 month earlier (October 1991) and would be down to 46% by January 1992. Table 2.5 also shows, hardly surprisingly, that no president during this period has been re-elected with an election day approval rating of below 52%. For a president to be re-elected in a landslide, he needs an approval rating on election day near or above 60%.

Table 2.5 Presidential approval 1 year before election day and on election day, 1948–2004

President seeking re-election (year)	Approval rating 1 year before election day	Approval rating on election day	Result of re-election bid
Harry Truman (1948)	54%	52%	Won
Dwight Eisenhower (1956)	78%	75%	Won
Richard Nixon (1972)	50%	62%	Won
Gerald Ford (1976)	**41%**	**45%**	**Lost**
Jimmy Carter (1980)	**32%**	**31%**	**Lost**
Ronald Reagan (1984)	53%	61%	Won
George H. W. Bush (1992)	**56%**	**34%**	**Lost**
Bill Clinton (1996)	52%	53%	Won
George W. Bush (2004)	54%	52%	Won

Figure 2.3 shows that Obama's job approval rating declined until late November of his first year, then remained pretty static — in the upper 40s — throughout the remainder of 2009 and right through to the start of 2011. There were then two brief peaks: one from mid-January to early March; the second through May 2011 coinciding with the killing of Osama bin Laden. But having reached just short of 53% approval by the end of May 2011, the next 6 months saw a steady decline to the low 40s by late October. Figure 2.4 shows that when looked at in 3-monthly instalments, Obama's job approval rating fell in each quarter throughout the first seven quarters of his presidency — that is from 20 January 2009 to 19 October 2010 — then picked up slightly in the 8th, 9th and 10th quarters (20 October 2010 to 19 July 2011) before falling sharply

in the 11th quarter (20 July to 19 October 2011). This is a worrying statistic for the President. The only modern day president with a lower 11th quarter approval rating was Jimmy Carter who lost his re-election bid the following year. To give this statistic some historical perspective, Obama's 11th quarter average of 41% ranks 220th out of the 262 quarters of presidential approval ratings since Gallup started publishing these data back in the days of President Truman (1945–53). In other words, it's bad.

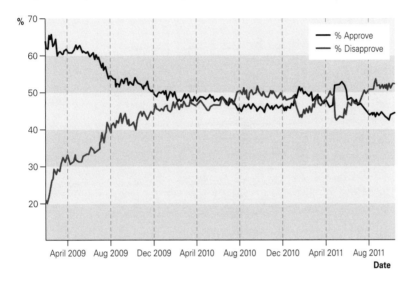

Figure 2.3 President Obama's job approval ratings, January 2009 to October 2011

Source: www.realclearpolitics.com

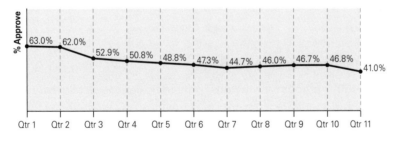

Figure 2.4 President Obama's job approval ratings, by quarters

Source: www.gallup.com

Possibly even more worrying news for the President was shown in data published by the website Five Thirty Eight (**www.fivethirtyeight.com**). This showed (Figure 2.5) that Obama lost support among almost every voting group during 2011, and most especially among the key groups which contributed to his election in 2008 — independents, Hispanics, the elderly, Midwesterners and women. Unless Obama can win back the support of these key groups, his re-election in November 2012 will be far from certain.

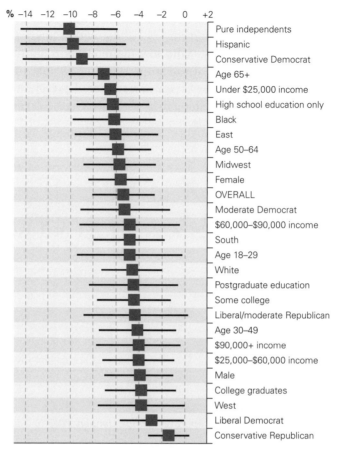

Figure 2.5 Change in approval rating for President Obama among key voting groups during 2011

Source: **www.fivethirtyeight.com**

Obama and the Electoral College

For all the opinion polls, straw polls, primaries, caucuses, television debates, fundraising and media excitement, in the end a presidential election comes down to the 538 votes in the Electoral College. (For a detailed explanation of how the Electoral College works, see my textbook, *US Government & Politics*, 3rd edition, Philip Allan Updates, 2009, pp. 91–97.) To win, Obama must gain an absolute majority (i.e. 270) of these Electoral College votes. In 2008, he won 365. Given that 48 of the 50 states award their Electoral College votes on a winner-takes-all basis, let's see how Obama is shaping up in the Electoral College a year before his re-election and which are likely to be the key 'swing' states in this election.

At this stage, I'm going to rule out a Carter-like collapse. (In 1980, President Carter won just 49 Electoral College votes, losing all but six states to Ronald

Reagan.) Obama, therefore, ought to be certain of winning the 15 states plus the District of Columbia which make up the fairly solid Democratic heartland — including California and New York — commanding 196 electoral votes. Likewise, the Republicans — barring a nominee who collapses — should be able to count on the Republican heartland of 21 states commanding 170 electoral votes. That leaves 14 states and 172 electoral votes in play.

In 2008, very few Democrats thought they could win Indiana, North Carolina or Missouri. They did win the first two, but the Republicans just held on to Missouri. It would seem possible at this stage that all three might go to the Republicans in 2012 — depending on who they choose as their nominee. Count another 36 electoral votes for the Republicans. So, the Republicans could expect to win 24 states with 206 electoral votes; the Democrats 15 states plus DC with 196 electoral votes. That leaves 11 states with 136 electoral votes in play.

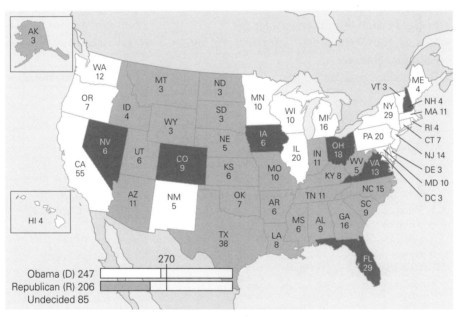

Figure 2.6 Electoral College forecast, 2012

Of these 11, four — Michigan (16), New Mexico (5), Pennsylvania (20) and Wisconsin (10) — really ought to end up in the Democratic column, unless Obama is struggling. So count another 51 electoral votes for the Democrats. That puts Obama on 247, just 23 votes short of victory (Figure 2.6). That leaves what are likely to be the seven true battleground states of 2012: Colorado (9), Florida (29), Iowa (6), Nevada (6), New Hampshire (4), Ohio (18) and Virginia (13). If this scenario played out, therefore, Obama would need to win only Florida of these key battleground states to secure a second term. Ohio and Virginia — both states won by Obama in 2008 — will also be key.

Exactly 1 year before election day, election analyst Nate Silver published an article in the *New York Times* entitled 'Is Obama toast? Handicapping the 2012 election'. At the end of the article he offered four possible scenarios, and for each he suggested Obama's chances of re-election:

- **Scenario 1:** Obama vs Romney; stagnant economy; Obama's approval rating on election day 43%: ***Obama 17%; Romney 83%.***
- **Scenario 2:** Obama vs Romney; improving economy; Obama's approval rating on election day 43%: ***Obama 60%; Romney 40%.***
- **Scenario 3:** Obama vs Perry; improving economy; Obama's approval rating on election day 43%: ***Obama 83%; Perry 17%.***
- **Scenario 4:** Obama vs Perry; stagnant economy; Obama's approval rating on election day 43%: ***Obama 41%; Perry 59%.***

This is how to keep yourself up-to-date with how Obama's re-election chances are looking:

- Watch the monthly US unemployment statistics, published on the first Friday of each month at **www.bls.gov**
- Watch the President's approval rating at **www.gallup.com** and **www.realclearpolitics.com**
- Watch state-by-state polling on the presidential race at **www.realclearpolitics.com**

Questions

1 Explain Rhodes Cook's comment on presidential re-election chances.
2 What does Table 2.1 tell us about recent presidential re-election rates?
3 Analyse the data presented in Table 2.2.
4 Why is unemployment looking like a worrying statistic for President Obama?
5 What conclusions can be drawn from state-by-state unemployment figures?
6 Analyse the data presented in Table 2.5.
7 What trends are discernible in President Obama's job approval ratings?
8 Name some key voting groups among which the President lost significant support during 2011.
9 What does Figure 2.6 tell us about Obama's re-election chances?

Chapter 3

The Republican's presidential nomination race

With no serious competition in the Democratic presidential nomination race in 2012, all eyes will be focused on the Republican contest. And as in 2008, the Republicans have an exceedingly open presidential nomination race: no incumbent president; no incumbent vice-president; no former vice-president, and this time around, not even an incumbent senator in sight. I'm also conscious that between my writing this chapter — in mid-November 2011 — and it being published, much may have changed.

The candidates

By 13 August 2011, there were 12 declared candidates for the Republican presidential nomination of 2012 (Table 3.1). By the following day there were only 11 as former-governor Tim Pawlenty became the first to drop out of the race. Pawlenty's early departure was a surprise as it was expected that he could have been a top tier candidate. Others will possibly withdraw even before the voting in the primaries and caucuses gets under way. Once we've got the results of the first four contests, the field will have thinned quite significantly. Will 2012 for the Republicans be a year like it was for them in 2008 when one candidate runs off with the nomination early on? Or will the Republicans in 2012 have a genuine contest?

Table 3.1 Republican presidential candidates 2012

Name	Current/last political post	Date formally announced (2011)	Date exited race (2011)
Gary Johnson	Ex-governor of New Mexico	21 April	
Newt Gingrich	House of Representatives	11 May	
Ron Paul	House of Representatives	13 May	
Herman Cain	[None]	21 May	3 December
Tim Pawlenty	Ex-governor of Minnesota	23 May	14 August
Mitt Romney	Ex-governor of Massachusetts	2 June	
Rick Santorum	Ex-senator (Pennsylvania)	6 June	
Michele Bachmann	House of Representatives	13 June	
Jon Huntsman	Ex-governor of Utah	21 June	
Thaddeus McCotter	House of Representatives	2 July	22 September
Buddy Roemer	Ex-governor of Louisiana	21 July	
Rick Perry	Governor of Texas	13 August	

The calendar

Table 3.2 Republican Party primary/caucus calendar, 2012

Date	State	Election type	Delegates
3 January	Iowa	Non-binding caucuses	28
10 January	†New Hampshire	Modified primary	12
21 January	†South Carolina	Open primary	25
31 January	†Florida	Closed primary	50
4 February	Nevada	Caucuses	28
7 February	Colorado	Non-binding caucuses	36
	Minnesota	Non-binding caucuses	40
	Missouri	Non-binding open primary	(see 17 March)
11 February	Maine	Non-binding caucuses	24
28 February	**†Arizona**	**Closed primary**	**29**
	†Michigan	Closed primary	30
3 March	Washington	Non-binding caucuses	43
6 March	Alaska	District conventions	27
(Super Tuesday)	Georgia	Modified primary	76
	Idaho	Caucuses	32
	Massachusetts	Modified primary	41
	North Dakota	Caucuses	28
	Ohio	Modified primary	66
	Oklahoma	Closed primary	43
	Tennessee	Open primary	58
	Vermont	Open primary	17
	Virginia	Open primary	50
6–10 March	Wyoming	Caucuses	29
10 March	Kansas	Caucuses	40
13 March	Alabama	Open primary	50
	Hawaii	Caucuses	20
	Mississippi	Open primary	40
17 March	Missouri	Caucuses	52
20 March	Illinois	Open primary	69
24 March	Louisiana	Closed primary	45
3 April	**District of Columbia**	**Closed primary**	**19**
	Maryland	Closed primary	37
	Texas	Open primary	155
	Wisconsin	Open primary	42
24 April	Connecticut	Closed primary	28
	Delaware	**Closed primary**	**17**
	New York	Closed primary	95
	Pennsylvania	Closed primary	72
	Rhode Island	Modified primary	19
8 May	Indiana	Open primary	46
	North Carolina	Modified primary	55
	West Virginia	Modified primary	31
15 May	Nebraska	Modified primary	35
	Oregon	Closed primary	28

Date	State	Election type	Delegates
22 May	Arkansas	Open primary	36
	Kentucky	Closed primary	45
5 June	California	Closed primary	172
	Montana	**Open primary**	**26**
	New Jersey	**Modified primary**	**50**
	New Mexico	Closed primary	23
	South Dakota	Closed primary	28
26 June	**Utah**	**Modified primary**	**40**

Note: winner-take-all primaries in bold. † Currently in violation of national party rules and therefore a 50% cut in delegates is shown

Total number of delegates: 2,288 (correct as of mid-December 2011)

Therefore number of delegate votes required for nomination: 1,145

Box 3.1 Mitt Romney

There is no doubt that this race is Mitt Romney's to lose. The Republican Party tends to be a deferential party — candidates are often nominated because it's 'their turn'. In 2008, the party nominated John McCain, the runner-up in the 2000 contest. And in 2012, the party may well nominate Mitt Romney, the runner-up in the 2008 contest. In 2008, Romney won 11 contests, including primaries in Massachusetts, Michigan and Colorado. He also had 11 second-place finishes, including New Hampshire, Florida and California. Romney served one term as governor of Massachusetts (2003–07), his signature achievement being the passage of the Massachusetts health reform law which did for his state much of what President Obama's 2010 healthcare reform law did for the nation as a whole. Romney's drawbacks include his previously liberal positions on some issues and his Mormon religion. His big plus is that polls show that of all the Republican candidates he has the best chance of beating the President. Romney turns 65 in March 2012.

After the relentless move to frontloading of the presidential nomination calendar in recent years, 2012 sees a significant change as a number of states have moved their primaries and caucuses to later in the season. More contests are scheduled for April, May and June than in any election cycle since 1992. This will be the longest nomination race — at least in terms of the calendar — running for 26 weeks from the Iowa caucuses on 3 January to the Utah primary on 26 June (Table 3.2). This has largely come about due to changes in party rules. Both parties set up commissions after the 2008 election to make recommendations for the 2012 nominating cycle. Both parties believed that the start to the primaries and caucuses was too early and that too many states were cramming their contests into too small a window too early in the year — in other words there was too much 'frontloading'. The Republican Temporary Delegate Selection Committee made certain recommendations and these were adopted by the Republican National Committee (RNC).

First, the Republican National Committee pushed back the potential start date of the contest. The RNC rules called for Iowa, New Hampshire, Nevada

and South Carolina to be allowed to hold their contests in February, but all the other states were to keep to a window between 6 March and 12 June. The 2008 contest had kicked off on 3 January and by 5 February 29 states had already held their primaries or caucuses; a further seven were held before the end of February. These 36 contests included all the ten largest states except Texas (4 March) and Pennsylvania (22 April). John McCain wrapped up the Republican nomination on 5 February just 5 weeks after the contest had started.

Second, they forbade any Republican state party from staging a winner-take-all contest before 1 April. In 2008, there were 17 Republican winner-take-all contests before that date which awarded huge numbers of delegates to the eventual nominee Senator John McCain (Table 3.3). McCain won 15 out of these 17 contests, thereby wrapping up the Republican nomination by 5 February. On that day, McCain won the contests in California and New York with 274 delegates between them. Yet McCain won only 42% of the vote in California with Romney not far behind on 35%. A proportional primary would have given a very different result.

Table 3.3 Winner-take-all primaries, 2008

Date	State	Number of delegates	Winner
15 January	Michigan	30	Romney
19 January	South Carolina	24	McCain
29 January	Florida	57	McCain
5 February	Arizona	53	McCain
	California	173	McCain
	Connecticut	30	McCain
	Georgia	72	Huckabee
	Missouri	58	McCain
	New York	101	McCain
	Oklahoma	41	McCain
12 February	District of Columbia	19	McCain
	Maryland	37	McCain
	Virginia	63	McCain
19 February	Wisconsin	40	McCain
4 March	Ohio	88	McCain
	Vermont	17	McCain
11 March	Mississippi	39	McCain

Not all the RNC plan was implemented. State parties guard their autonomy jealously and the 2012 nomination season in the end opened on exactly the same date as it did 4 years ago. But after that, the pace will be much slower. Super Tuesday, which saw 21 Republican contests on 6 February in 2008, will feature just 10 Republican contests and will occur a month later in 2012. Some large states with large numbers of delegates at stake have moved their contests to later in the cycle: New York has moved from 5 February (2008) to 24 April (2012); California from 5 February (2008) to 5 June (2012). The 37th Republican contest, which occurred on 19 February in 2008, will occur on 24 April in 2012. The number of winner-take-all primaries has fallen from 17 to just 6.

The contests

Table 3.2 shows the different types of contests being held during the Republican nomination cycle this year. Here's a quick run-down on these different types of contests:

- **Primary:** a state-based election to choose a party's presidential candidate. A presidential primary shows support for a candidate among ordinary voters and often also chooses delegates committed to vote for that candidate at the National Party Convention.
- **Caucuses:** a state-based series of meetings to choose a party's candidate for the presidency. They fulfil the same functions as primaries.
- **Open primary:** a primary in which any registered voter can vote in the primary of either party.
- **Closed primary:** a primary in which only registered Republicans can vote in the Republican primary, and only registered Democrats can vote in the Democratic primary.
- **Modified primary:** a primary in which registered Republicans can vote only in the Republican primary, and registered Democrats can vote only in the Democratic primary, but those registered as independents may vote in either party's primary.
- **Non-binding primary/caucus:** a primary or caucus in which delegates are not selected, i.e. the delegates eventually chosen are not bound by the result of the primary/caucus. This is sometimes referred to as a 'beauty contest' or 'preference vote'.
- **Winner-take-all primary:** a primary in which the winner of the primary is awarded all that state's delegates.
- **Proportional primary:** a primary in which delegates are awarded in proportion to the votes that each candidate wins. Most states set a threshold — a minimum percentage of votes that a candidate must receive to get any of the state's delegates; this is usually set at 15% of the vote.

The reason why a number of the early primaries and caucuses are 'non-binding' is to avoid breaking the Republican National Committee rules for 2012 which state:

> **Rule 15(b):** No primary to elect, select, allocate, or bind delegates to the national convention shall occur prior to Tuesday 6 March 2012, except Iowa, New Hampshire, South Carolina and Nevada [which] may begin their processes any time on or after 1 February 2012.

> **Rule 16(a):** If a state party violates the timing rules, the number of delegates from that state is reduced by 50%.

Once the Florida state Republican Party had decided to hold its primary on 31 January, in contravention of these rules, Iowa, New Hampshire and South Carolina leapfrogged over them in order to preserve their 'first in the nation' privilege. Iowa avoided having its delegation cut in half by holding a non-binding contest, meaning that the votes cast in the Iowa caucuses on 3 January did not directly choose any delegates to the Republican National Convention. But New Hampshire and South Carolina opted to hold a delegate selection primary and forego half their delegate allocation. The two other states which have violated the rules are Arizona and Michigan. Both scheduled delegate selection primaries before the 6 March date laid down in Rule 15(b). Arizona further violated the rules by scheduling a winner-take-all primary before 1 April. It was unclear at the time of writing whether further sanctions would be taken against the Arizona state party. Missouri avoided being penalised by holding a non-binding primary on 7 February — outside the permitted window — but choosing its delegates in caucuses held on 17 March which was within the permitted window: clever but confusing. All this shows the difficulty there is in the national parties getting state parties to toe the line when it comes to such matters — another price of a federal system of government.

The invisible primary

The invisible primary is the time between candidates declaring an intention to run for the presidency and the first contests in the primary season. This roughly approximates to the calendar year before the presidential election itself. The first candidate declaration came unusually late in this cycle. Indeed for the first time that I can remember, the incumbent president declared his candidacy for re-election before a single challenger from the other party. President Obama formally launched his re-election campaign on 4 April 2011 while the first Republican challenger — former New Mexico governor Gary Johnson — did not throw his hat into the ring until 21 April.

The term 'invisible primary' is somewhat misleading nowadays. Back in the 1970s when the term was first used, it was an apt description of the pre-election year for there was very little if anything to see — hence 'invisible'. But nowadays there is a great deal to see — probably far too much — and what there is to see is, I would argue, of dubious importance or relevance. There is quite a bit of evidence to suggest that the mushrooming of 'events' during the so-called invisible primary is more to cater for the needs of the 24/7 news channels than to assist the voters with selecting well-qualified presidential candidates. Let's take two examples.

In early August of the year before the election, Iowa Republicans stage the Ames Straw Poll. Ames is a small town of less than 60,000 people in central Iowa. It's about the size of Guildford in Surrey or Taunton in Somerset — though slightly smaller than both. The Ames Straw Poll event, which lasts all day, is a cross between a fun fair and a political fundraising event. There are barbecues, stalls for any candidates who want to set one up, and a speaking slot given to each candidate who attends. Here's a description of the 2011 event from *The Economist* magazine:

> The atmosphere of the event is more carnival than campaign rally. Candidates lay on food and entertainment to try to lure supporters to the venue. They even provide buses to ferry in adoring followers from the furthest corners of the state. Many of the punters appear to have come more for the free food and fun day out than for the vote itself. Children leapt about on bouncy castles like politicians jockeying for attention. One participant even admitted to being a Democrat who had come simply to hear Buddy Holly's former band, which was playing for Rick Santorum.

The winner of the 2011 Ames Straw Poll was Congresswoman Michele Bachmann who, as a result, garnered huge media publicity and significant increases both in her poll ratings and campaign bank balance. She received 28% of the votes, just a point ahead of another House member, Ron Paul. Yet for all the hours of media coverage and the miles of newspaper columns filled, just 16,892 people voted. It decides absolutely nothing. And it is a well-known fact that the folk who turn up at this event are not even representative of those who attend the Iowa caucuses 5 months later — and we know how unrepresentative they are of national Republican voters. Here's *The Economist* again:

> Straw poll participants tend to be more religious and more conservative than Republican primary voters. Candidates with small but devoted followings, like Ron Paul, a libertarian from Texas, can do well. Mr Paul was placed second, just one percentage point behind Mrs Bachmann, but pundits still put his chances of winning the [Republican presidential] nomination at next-to-nothing.

At the 2007 Ames Straw Poll, the eventual Republican presidential nominee — Senator John McCain — got less than 1% of the vote. On that occasion the Straw Poll was won by Mitt Romney. Five months later, however, the Iowa Republican caucuses were won by former Arkansas governor Mike Huckabee. Neither got anywhere close to winning the party's presidential nomination.

If the Ames Straw Poll is of dubious worth, much the same can be said about the seemingly endless series of televised debates which take place between the party candidates during this so-called invisible primary season. There will have been a total of 16 televised debates between the first on 5 May 2011 and the Iowa caucuses on 3 January 2012, 13 of them coming in a 15-week period between early September and mid-December. *Saturday Night Live*, a reliable source of political satire, soon started poking fun at this phenomenon with its own spoof version. Again, one can rightly ask, as with the Ames

Straw Poll, what is the point of it? With up to nine candidates on stage at the same time, the tone meanders alarmingly from boredom to farce. Here's how Charles Kesler saw it in a recent column on the website RealClearPolitics (**www.realclearpolitics.com**, 'Debating the debates', 21 October 2011):

> For an office designed with George Washington in mind, debating skills were never a high priority. The president is commander-in-chief of the armed forces; has the power to make treaties and appoint ambassadors, Supreme Court justices and cabinet officers; and wields the veto pen and issues pardons and reprieves at his discretion. But none of these or his other constitutional powers and duties require him to debate anyone.

In a parliamentary system such as the UK, where the prime minister needs debating skills on a weekly basis at question time, it might make sense to require such skills in those aspiring to the office. But it is hard to see what relevance such skills have to being an effective and competent president. Kesler continues:

> With one minute for answers, 30 seconds for rebuttals, preening questioners trying to outshine the candidates, additional queries pouring in on Facebook, Twitter and Google, if anything resembling a debate takes place in these Republican circles of hell, it's a miracle. So why do we tune in? Perhaps to learn a little something about the candidates and the issues, or more likely so we'll get the jokes on *Saturday Night Live*.

Not a typical race

The 2012 Republican nomination race is far from typical. Let's consider five ways in which the build-up to the race was untypical.

An unusually late start

First, it has been an unusually late-starting and slow-developing nomination race. In the run-up to the 2008 election, the first Democrat declared his candidacy in December 2006, the first Republican on 11 January 2007. By mid-February 2007 there were a further six Democrats and five Republicans in the race. By the equivalent date in 2011 there were no declared candidates at all. Even in the run-up to the 2004 election — similar to 2012 in that an incumbent president was running for re-election — the first candidate for the challenging party declared on 13 January 2003. In this election cycle, the first candidate from the challenging party emerged 3 months later.

A large number of high-profile Republicans chose not to run

Second, it has been unusual because a large number of high-profile Republicans talked about running but then chose not to. 'I'm not running for president in 2012. Period,' stated Governor Bobby Jindal of Louisiana, on 16 November 2010. 'I will not be a candidate for president next year,' was how Governor

Haley Barbour of Mississippi made his announcement on 25 April 2011. 'All the factors say "go", but my heart says "no",' was ex-governor Mike Huckabee's way of putting it on 14 May. 'Now is not my time,' announced Governor Chris Christie of New Jersey on 4 October after many had pleaded with him to run. And there were other notable non-runners: Senator John Thune of South Dakota (22 February 2011); Governor Mitch Daniels of Indiana (22 May); and Florida's ex-governor Jeb Bush. Even Sarah Palin and Donald Trump passed up the chance of further self-publicity. It's been like the Democratic race back in 1992 when big names like Al Gore, Bill Bradley, Dick Gephardt and Mario Cuomo all chose not to run.

No dominant front-runner in the polls
Third, there has been no dominant front-runner in the polls. Although Mitt Romney has generally been leading many polls and has been described in the media as 'the front-runner', the Gallup polling organisation described him as one of the weakest front-runners in any recent Republican nomination race. In the poll-of-polls posted on the RealClearPolitics website showing the average of polls between March 2010 and November 2011, Romney only once got higher than 25% — 25.5% in late-October 2011 — but by that time he was in second place behind Herman Cain. Dan Balz pointed out in a *Washington Post* column ('Yes, the Republican race is a strange campaign', 5 November 2011) that by this time seven different people had led the Republican race in one or more polls: Romney, Huckabee, Trump, Palin, former New York mayor Rudy Giuliani, Perry and Cain. By the end of November former House Speaker Newt Gringrich was leading the polls — the eighth person to do so.

Fundraising was much slower than usual
Fourth, fundraising has been much slower than in the 2008 election cycle. By the end of September 2007, the Republican candidates had raised collectively about $230 million. Mitt Romney alone had raised $85 million by then. That figure of $85 million was the collective total of all the Republican candidates by the end of September 2011, by which time Romney had raised just $44 million.

The pace of the campaign was much slower than usual
Fifth, the campaign has been much slower than 4 years ago, with less campaigning, fewer visits to key states, and fewer offices opened in these states. Four years ago, between 1 July and 1 November, the leading Republican threesome of Huckabee, Romney and McCain spent a combined 48 days in New Hampshire and 66 days in Iowa. This time around during the same period, the leading threesome of Romney, Perry and Cain collectively spent just 37 days in New Hampshire and only 23 days in Iowa. By November 2007, Barack Obama had opened 30 offices in Iowa. By November 2011, Rick Perry had opened just five offices in Iowa, with Romney and Cain having opened just one each.

Box 3.2 lists some key events to watch out for as election year progresses.

Box 3.2	Some key election year events to watch out for
6 March	Super Tuesday
Mid-August	Expect the Republican nominee to announce his running mate
27–30 August	Republican National Convention in Tampa, Florida
3–7 September	Democratic National Convention in Charlotte, North Carolina
3 October	First presidential debate: Denver, Colorado
11 October	Vice-presidential debate: Danville, Kentucky
16 October	Second presidential debate: Hempstead, New York
22 October	Third presidential debate: Boca Raton, Florida
6 November	Election day
17 December	Electoral College voting in state capitals

What to watch in 2012

Of the first four Republican contests in 2012 — Iowa, New Hampshire, South Carolina and Florida — which has the best track record at picking the party's presidential candidate? We will answer the question by looking at the last six closely contested Republican nominations: 1976, 1980, 1988, 1996, 2000 and 2008. In 1984, 1992 and 2004, all the Republican contests were won by the incumbent president.

Table 3.4 Winners in Iowa, New Hampshire, South Carolina and Florida,
1976–2008 (selected)

Year	1976	1980	1988	1996	2000	2008
Nominee	Ford	Reagan	Bush	Dole	Bush	McCain
Iowa	Ford	Bush	Dole	Dole	Bush	Huckabee
New Hampshire	Ford	Reagan	Bush	Buchanan	McCain	McCain
South Carolina	Reagan	Reagan	Bush	Dole	Bush	McCain
Florida	Ford	Reagan	Bush	Dole	Bush	McCain

'Every four years, the road to the White House runs through Exira and towns like it across Iowa because of the state's crucial role in the presidential nomination process.' So wrote Andrew Ward in the *Financial Times* in October 2007. Was he right? Is Iowa a good picker of Republican presidential candidates? How many times in these six election cycles did Iowa pick the Republican winner? Answer: only three times — 1976 (Ford), 1996 (Dole) and 2000 (Bush). And only Bush in 2000 went on to win the White House — not a great record.

'The road to the White House runs through New Hampshire.' So claims much political folklore in general, and the website blurb of Gary Johnson, one of this year's Republican wannabes, in particular. So how many times in these six cycles did New Hampshire pick the Republican winner? Answer: just four times, but it's got it wrong in two of the last three — 1996 when it went for Pat Buchanan, not Bob Dole; and in 2000 when it went for John McCain, not George W. Bush. Only twice — 1980 (Reagan) and 1988 (Bush) — has New Hampshire's Republican winner gone on to win both the nomination and the presidency. So it's got a better record than Iowa, but hardly fail safe.

South Carolina's record in picking the Republican nominee is pretty good. In fact, it's picked the winner in every contest since 1980. In 1976, it got it wrong when it picked Reagan over Ford. But Florida can go one better, picking the Republican winner in all six contests since 1976: Ford, Reagan, Bush, Dole, Bush and McCain. So while the media will focus on Iowa and New Hampshire — the traditional 'first in the nation' contests — more shrewd students of presidential politics will keep their eye to the south, to South Carolina and Florida when it comes to looking for clues to picking Republican Party nominees.

Another important factor to watch out for as the primaries and caucuses play out is the turnout. When comparing turnout with the 2008 primaries, it will be possible to compare turnout only in those states that are holding their contests at a comparable time to 4 years ago. Table 3.5 shows seven states that one might watch — five which saw an increase from 2000 to 2008 and two which saw a decrease. High turnout in primaries generally shows a highly motivated electorate which, were it to occur, would bode well for Republicans in November.

Table 3.5 Turnout in selected Republican primaries, 2000 and 2008 compared

State	2000 turnout	2008 turnout
New Hampshire	238,206	238,328
Arizona	322,669	451,584
Georgia	643,188	958,399
Texas	1,126,757	1,384,663
Mississippi	114,979	143,286
Michigan	1,276,770	868,083
South Carolina	573,101	443,203

In the 2008 nominating contests, both parties' front-runners — Democrat Hillary Clinton and Republican Rudy Giuliani — failed to win their respective nominations. Less than a month before the Iowa caucuses, Hillary Clinton led Barack Obama in the Democratic race by 18 percentage points in the Gallup Poll (14–16 December). In the same poll, Rudy Giuliani led John McCain by 13 points in the Republican race. Thus the conventional wisdom — that the winner of the invisible primary goes on to win the nomination — was turned on its head. Will 2012 have been another year for an upset, or will conventional wisdom have re-established itself?

Box 3.3 lists some of the best websites to go to for following the progress of the 2012 election.

Box 3.3 Some of the best websites for following the election

- www.realclearpolitics.com
- www.washingtonpost.com
- www.nytimes.com
- www.thegreenpapers.com
- www.fivethirtyeight.blogs.nytimes.com
- www.centerforpolitics.org/crystalball
- www.electoral-vote.com
- www.politico.com
- www.pollingreport.com
- www.gallup.com

Questions

1 What is 'frontloading'? To what extent was the movement towards 'front-loading' reversed in 2012?
2 What changes in the rules regarding the nomination process did the Republican National Committee propose for 2012?
3 Explain the differences between an open primary, a closed primary and a modified primary.
4 What criticisms can be made of the importance attached to the Ames Straw Poll?
5 Why does Charles Kesler think that the candidate debates during this period are of questionable use and relevance?
6 What five reasons are given to suggest that the build-up to the 2012 Republican nomination race was untypical?
7 Which state has the best record of picking Republican presidential nominees?

Chapter 4

US parties: why are the differences now 'between' rather than 'within'?

In days gone by, everyone quoted D. W. Brogan on US political parties when he said that they were 'like two bottles with different labels, both empty'. The conventional wisdom was that the differences *within* the two parties were far more significant than the differences *between* them. And as recently as 1997, Mark Shields writing in the *Washington Post* famously remarked that 'as of today, the country basically has two Republican parties, separated by the issue of abortion'.

But writing just a decade later in his landmark book *The Second Civil War* (2007), Ronald Brownstein had this to say of the new era of what he termed 'hyper-partisanship' in US politics:

> The defining characteristics of this age are greater unity *within* the parties and more distinct conflicts *between* them. On almost every major issue, the distance between the two parties has widened, even as dissent within the parties has diminished.

This marks a profound change. So what did the two major parties in the USA used to look like? What do they look like today? Why and how did the change come about? And what are the consequences of these changes?

The way things were

One of the simplest ways to understand what's happened to the Democrats and Republicans is to take two snapshots of the US Senate. Being the small body that it is — just 100 members — it's more manageable to look at this than try to study the country as a whole. So let's go back to the Senate 30 years ago and see what we find by studying the voting records of senators in 1982 (Figure 4.1).

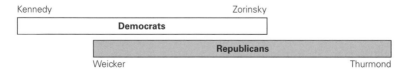

Figure 4.1 The parties in the Senate, 1982

In that year, the most liberal of the Senate Democrats was Ted Kennedy of Massachusetts, while the most conservative of the Senate Democrats was Ed Zorinsky of Nebraska. They rarely voted together, yet they were both Democrats. Among Republicans in the Senate in 1982, the most liberal or 'moderate' Republican was Lowell Weicker of Connecticut. In the same party was conservative Strom Thurmond of South Carolina. Again, Weicker and Thurmond had little in common — except they were both Republicans. Between Weicker — the most liberal Republican — and Zorinsky — the most conservative Democrat — were 35 Democrats and 23 Republicans. In other words, 35 Democrats were more conservative than Weicker and 23 Republicans were more liberal than Zorinsky. Republican Strom Thurmond was more likely to vote with Democrat Ed Zorinsky than with fellow Republican Lowell Weicker. Likewise, Democrat Ted Kennedy was more likely to vote with Republican Lowell Weicker than with fellow Democrat Ed Zorinsky. As Figure 4.1 shows, there was a huge ideological overlap between the two parties. The differences *within* the parties were far greater than the differences *between* them.

The way things are

Now let's move from 1982 to 2010 and we shall see what a profound change has taken place within the parties (Figure 4.2). In 2010, the most liberal Senate Democrat was Patrick Leahy of Vermont and the most conservative of the Senate Democrats was Ben Nelson of Nebraska. Among Republicans in the Senate in 2010, the most liberal or 'moderate' Republican was George Voinovich of Ohio and the most conservative of the Senate Republicans was Jim DeMint of South Carolina.

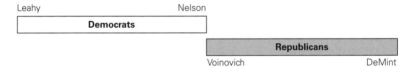

Figure 4.2 The parties in the Senate, 2010

Between Voinovich — the most liberal Republican — and Nelson — the most conservative Democrat — there was not a single senator. In other words, all 40 Republicans were more conservative than Ben Nelson and all 60 Democrats were more liberal than George Voinovich. As Figure 4.2 shows, there was absolutely no ideological overlap at all between the two parties. The differences *between* the parties are now greater than the differences *within* them. Both parties have become more ideologically cohesive and distinct: the Democrats have become a more distinctly and cohesive liberal party; the Republicans have become a more distinctly and cohesive conservative party.

Why things changed

So why did things change so dramatically over such a comparatively short time? We are going to consider six reasons.

The breakup of the Solid South

For over a century following the Civil War (1861–65), people living in the South followed the rule of 'vote as you shot'. As the Democratic Party was the party of the South in the Civil War — the Republicans were the party of the Union (the north) — that meant that almost everyone in the South voted Democrat, hence the term 'the Solid South'. The South remained solidly Democrat until well into the last quarter of the twentieth century.

In the 1976 presidential election (Figure 4.3), the South was still pretty solidly Democrat. Jimmy Carter, the Democrat candidate, won 10 of the 11 southern states — all except Virginia. This made both parties — and especially the Democrats — a strange ideological mix. The Democrats garnered support from the South — the most politically conservative region of the USA — as well as from the liberal northeast and Great Lakes region. The Republicans, on the other hand, controlled the conservative heartland stretching from Montana and North Dakota to Arizona and Kansas, as well as still keeping significant support in more liberal parts of the northeast — New Jersey and Connecticut for example.

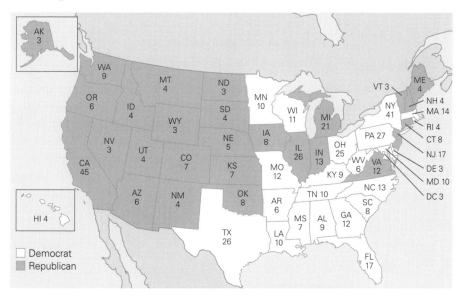

Figure 4.3 Presidential election, 1976

Source: www.270towin.com

But six elections later — in 2000 — one can see (Figure 4.4) that there had been a complete ideological sorting out of the parties' regional support. Most notably, the Solid (Democrat) South had collapsed and was now solidly Republican. This ideological sorting out meant that the two parties became more cohesive: the Southern conservatives' move to the Republican Party left the Democrats a more cohesively liberal party and made the Republicans a more cohesively conservative party. The Republicans were now too conservative for their former 'moderate' wing — in the west and the northeast — and these regions gravitated to the Democrats.

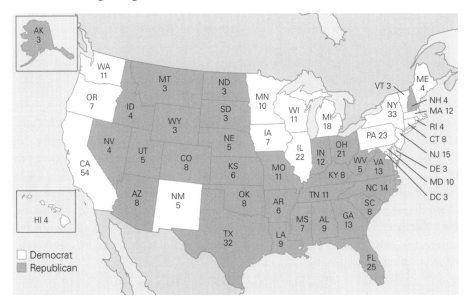

Figure 4.4 Presidential election, 2000

Source: **www.270towin.com**

And all this wasn't happening only at the presidential level. It was happening in congressional and state elections too, as Table 4.1 clearly shows. In 1960, a century after the start of the Civil War, the South was still solidly Democrat: 99 of the 106 southern House members were Democrats, as were all 22 southern senators and all 11 southern governors. Twenty years later — in the year we took our snapshot of the Senate (1982) — some cracks had begun to appear, especially in the Senate, but the South was still overwhelmingly Democrat. But in the last 30 years, the breakup has become complete. Today, 94 (71%) of the 132 southern House members are Republicans. The Democrats have only six southerners remaining in the Senate and control only two of the southern governorships. It's an almost complete reversal.

Table 4.1 Breakup of the Solid South, 1960–2010

Year	House (D–R)	Senate (D–R)	Governors (D–R)
1960	99–7	22–0	11–0
1982	82–34	11–11	9–2
2010	38–94	6–16	2–9

Notice, too, that the number of House members was 106 in 1960, 116 in 1982 and 132 by 2010. This shows that the South has had the fastest growing population in the country. More voters means more House seats; more House seats means more Electoral College votes in the presidential election — 128 in 1960 but 154 in 2008; and all this means more political clout. It's been very good news for the Republican Party and largely accounts for why it has done so well in both presidential and congressional elections in the past two decades.

Party switching

Not only did voters switch but some politicians did too, contributing further to the ideological cohesion of both parties. A number of conservative Democrats switched to become Republicans, and a smaller number of liberal Republicans switched to become Democrats. Three of the biggest names in the Republican Party during the final decades of the twentieth century were Ronald Reagan (President 1981–89), Strom Thurmond (Senator 1956–2003) and Trent Lott (House member: 1973–89; Senator 1989–2007). All three began their political lives as Democrats. Box 4.1 shows nine Democrat members of Congress who have switched to the Republican Party during the past 30 years — significantly all southerners.

Box 4.1	Party switchers: Democrat to Republicans		
1983	Rep. Phil Gramm (Texas)	1995	Rep. Nathan Deal (Georgia)
1994	Sen. Richard Shelby (Alabama)	1995	Rep. Mike Parker (Mississippi)
1995	Rep. Jimmy Hayes (Louisiana)	2002	Rep. Virgil Goode (Virginia)
1995	Rep. Greg Laughlin (Texas)	2009	Rep. Parker Griffith (Alabama)
1995	Rep. Billy Tauzin (Louisiana)		

The most prominent party switcher of late in the other direction was Senator Arlen Specter of Pennsylvania who in 2009, after nearly 30 years as a Republican senator, switched to the Democratic Party. Specter had fallen out of favour with Republicans — both at the national and state level — because of his liberal views. But the following year, Specter lost in the Democratic Senate primary to a more liberal Democrat. Box 4.2 shows the four other Republican members of Congress who switched to the Democrats during the past three decades — significantly three of the five were from the northeast. With conservative Democrats joining the Republicans and liberal Republicans joining the Democrats, one can see how this contributes to greater ideological cohesion within the two parties and sharper differences between them.

Box 4.2	Party switchers: Republican to Democrat
1985	(now) Rep. John Yarmuth (Kentucky)
1996	(now) Rep. Carolyn McCarthy (New York)
1999	Rep. Michael Forbes (New York)
2006	(now) Sen. Jim Webb (Virginia)
2009	Sen. Arlen Specter (Pennsylvania)

Redistricting

After each 10-yearly census in the USA, many states need to redraw the boundaries of their districts which elect members to the House of Representatives in order to ensure equal population in each district. This process is called redistricting. In most states this process is controlled by politicians who therefore draw the district boundaries to enhance political advantage.

In a number of states, redistricting following the 2000 census was done in order to facilitate as many safe seats as possible — for both parties. Take, for example, California. Following the 2000 census, California would have 53 House seats. In the 2010 mid-term elections, the average vote for House winners in California was 66%. That means the average vote for the loser was 34% — a 32 percentage-point margin. Now imagine you are a California Democrat who has just won re-election by 32 percentage points. How much notice do you need to take of Republican voters? Not a lot. (The same, of course, goes for California House Republicans and their regard for the views of Democrat constituents.) If one defines a competitive district as one in which the margin of the winner is 10 percentage points or less, then only 4 (8%) of the 53 California House races were competitive in 2010. The other 49 California House members, therefore, have little or no incentive to talk or vote in a bipartisan fashion. Indeed, cooperation and compromise with the other party might well get them into trouble with their partisan supporters back home. All these House members need to do is to appeal to the party base — that means operating in a strictly partisan and ideological fashion. This is a third factor which has increased the ideological cohesion of the parties.

Voters who are more ideological

It's not just the politicians who have become more partisan and ideological; it's the voters as well. Indeed, this is something of a chicken-and-egg argument: do ideological politicians lead to more ideological voting, or does increased ideological voting lead to more ideological politicians? One way to see the way in which voters have become more ideological is to see the decrease there has been over recent decades in split-ticket voting (Figure 4.5). Split-ticket voting is the practice of voting for candidates of two or more parties for different offices at the same election. So, for example, one might at the same election vote for the Democratic presidential candidate but a Republican senator, or a Republican House member but a Democratic senator. Split-ticket voting indicates that the voter has only a loose attachment to a political party.

The opposite of split-ticket voting is straight-ticket voting where one votes for the candidates of the same party for all the offices on the ballot at any given election. Straight-ticket voting indicates that the voter has a strong partisan attachment. So if split-ticket voting declines, partisanship is likely to have increased. This is exactly what has happened. Whereas in 1972, 30% of voters split their tickets, by 2008 this figure was just 17%.

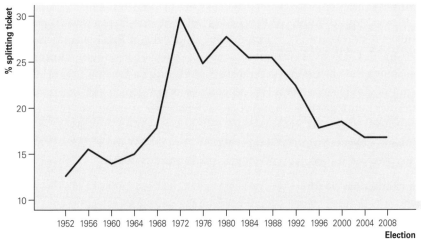

Figure 4.5 Split-ticket voting, 1952–2008

Source: www.gallup.com

Presidents who are 'dividers' rather than 'unifiers'

Adverts for Marmite say that 'you either love it or you hate it'. If that's true, then in the past two decades we have moved from the imperial presidency to the Marmite presidency. For presidents, who tended to be unifying figures, have become increasingly divisive. 'I'm a uniter, not a divider,' claimed George W. Bush running for president in 2000. Few would agree that his presidency bore this out. Like Clinton before him and Obama after him, Bush proved to be a divisive president: like Marmite, you either loved him or hated him.

Table 4.2 shows presidential approval by party from Eisenhower to Obama. Now of course one would expect Republican president Dwight Eisenhower to be more popular among Republicans than Democrats; likewise you would expect Democrat John Kennedy to be more popular among Democrats than Republicans — and they were. But what has changed is the gap in the approval levels between the president's own party and the other party.

Table 4.2 Presidential partisan approval: Eisenhower to Obama

President	Republican approval (%)	Democrat approval (%)	Approval gap (percentage points)
Eisenhower	87	55	32
Kennedy	58	87	29
Johnson	64	83	19
Nixon	82	48	34
Ford	66	38	28
Carter	46	72	26
Reagan	84	39	45
George H. W. Bush	83	51	32
Clinton	23	75	52
George W. Bush	92	47	45
Obama	23	88	65

In previous decades even voters who were not of the president's party still thought quite highly of him. After all, 48% of Democrats approved of President Nixon and 46% of Republicans approved of President Carter. That's all changed. Only 23% of Republicans approved of President Clinton — the same figure that in 2009–10 approved of President Obama. The right-hand column of Table 4.2 shows the percentage point gap in the approval rating of the two major parties' supporters. Whereas the average gap for presidents Eisenhower through Carter was 28 percentage points, the average gap for presidents Reagan through Obama was 48 percentage points. Americans' view of their president has clearly become much more partisan.

Rise of the new media

Finally, US political parties have become far more ideologically cohesive and distinctive as a result of the rise of the new media. Back in the 1960s and 1970s, Americans gleaned most of their political news and opinion from the old media — essentially terrestrial television in the shape of ABC, CBS and NBC. That's all there was. Whoever you were, wherever you lived and whatever your political opinion, you watched, for example, Walter Cronkite — the presenter of *CBS Evening News* for almost two decades until his retirement in 1981. What the old media offered was a middle-of-the-road commentary on US politics: you heard good and bad about Democrats and Republicans. 'Uncle Walter', as Cronkite was affectionately known, was described as 'the most trusted man in America'.

Hardly a description one would associate with a new media figure like Fox News' Glenn Beck. Today, the old media has been deposed and replaced by the new media. In terms of television news, that means such channels as CNN, MSNBC and Fox News each giving their own distinct ideological slant on politics. Few Republicans will be found regularly tuning in to CNN or MSNBC; few Democrats will be devotees of Fox News.

Not only do today's Americans tune in to watch only the news network which suits their beliefs and prejudices, but the same is true of the way they use and sample the other sources of new media, such as Talk Radio, the internet and blogging. What they see and read is not an updated version of Uncle Walter but more like the political equivalent of World Wrestling Entertainment. And all this is very new — as Box 4.3 clearly shows.

Box 4.3	The rise of the new media

- CNN (1980)
- Talk Radio (early 1990s)
- Internet (1991)
- Text messaging (1992)
- Blogging (1997)
- Facebook (2004)
- YouTube (2005)
- Twitter (2006)

Implications for government

Over recent decades, therefore, there has been a profound change in the characteristics of US political parties. No longer is it just the labels which are different, to paraphrase Brogan, but the contents. Both parties have become more ideologically cohesive and distinct. No longer can they be described as 'decentralised, undisciplined and non-ideological'. They are now much more centralised, well disciplined and distinctively ideological. They are much more like the disciplined parties of a parliamentary form of government, such as the UK.

But the high levels of party discipline that we now see in Congress have serious implications for government. Gone are the old-fashioned ideas of compromise, bipartisanship and 'reaching across the aisle' to work with politicians on the other side. The other party is now seen not so much as your opponent but as your enemy. Gone too is the era of civility in which politicians from both sides of the aisle — and their families — fraternised on evenings and weekends. Most members of Congress are now in Washington for only 3 days a week — Tuesday through Thursday — spending the long weekend back in their states and districts. No opportunity now, therefore, for games of golf or supper parties in Georgetown, Washington's select suburb. All this combines to make divided government — with one party controlling the presidency while the other party controls Congress — much more difficult to work, a factor which may well come into play once again in January 2013.

Questions

1 Explain how the comments of Brogan and Brownstein differ.
2 (a) Explain what is shown in Figures 4.1 and 4.2. (b) What are the implications of these differences?
3 What happened to party support in the South between 1960 and 2010?
4 What is the significance of the data shown in Boxes 4.1 and 4.2?
5 Explain what redistricting is and how it has contributed to increased partisanship.
6 What does Figure 4.5 show? Why is this significant?
7 Analyse and explain the data presented in Table 4.2.
8 How has the political role played by the media changed in recent decades?
9 What implications does increased partisanship have for governing the USA?

Chapter 5

Initiatives, referendums and recall elections

What you need to know

- An **initiative**, otherwise known as a proposition, is a mechanism by which citizens of a state can place proposed laws — and in some states, constitutional amendments — on the state ballot.
- Voters in 24 states have such a mechanism.
- A **referendum** is an electoral device by which voters can effectively veto a bill passed by the state legislature.
- Voters in all 50 states have such a device.
- A **recall election** enables voters in a state to remove an elected official from office before their term has expired.
- Voters in 19 states, plus the District of Columbia, have such a mechanism.

The story so far

The first initiative (or proposition) was put to the voters of the state of Oregon in 1904. From that date through to the elections of 2010, a total of 2,356 initiatives have been placed on state ballots, of which 960 (41%) have been approved. But as Figure 5.1 clearly shows, it is in the last two decades that this manifestation of direct democracy has really come into its own, with over 700 proposed and 300 approved since 1990. The record year for initiatives on the ballot was 1996 with 93, followed by 2006 (79), 2000 (76) and 1994 (71).

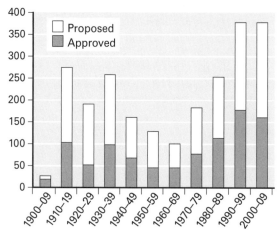

Figure 5.1 Number of initiatives per decade
Source: www.iandrinstitute.org

In terms of which states have made the most use of initiatives, Figure 5.2 shows that Oregon and California lead the way, followed by Colorado, North Dakota, Arizona and Washington state. That list of six states has a geographical pattern to it (Figure 5.3). Three — Washington, Oregon and California — are on the Pacific coast, Arizona and Colorado are in the Mountain West, while North Dakota is in the West North Central region. All six are well west of the Mississippi, and all six are far removed from Washington DC. Whereas all three states which border the Pacific are in the top six initiative users, only three of the 14 states which border the Atlantic — Florida, Maine and Massachusetts — even use the initiative, and none feature among the league leaders.

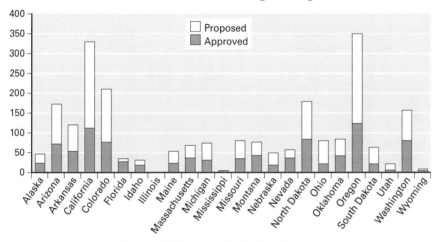

Figure 5.2 Number of initiatives by state

Source: www.iandrinstitute.org

Figure 5.3 The USA by region

What happened in 2010?

In 2010, there were 42 initiatives on the ballot: 18 (43%) were approved and 24 were rejected. This figure of 42 was the lowest in mid-term election years since 1986. There were a further 118 state-wide ballot measures in 2010 making a total of 160 in all, involving voters in 37 states (Figure 5.4).

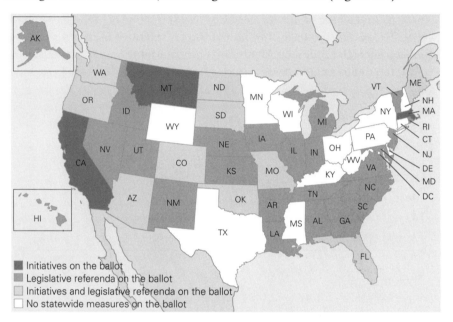

Figure 5.4 Initiatives and referendums on state ballots, 2010
Source: **www.ncsl.org**

The 2010 mid-terms saw Republicans in the ascendancy and therefore it was likely to be a good year too for voters with conservative views. Whereas in 2006 — the previous set of mid-term elections — just 32% of voters described themselves as 'conservative', in 2010 that figure was 41%. And the results of votes on initiatives showed a good deal of success for conservatives.

- **Medical use of marijuana:** rejected in all four states that had it on the ballot: California, Arizona, Oregon and South Dakota. Up to 2008, 12 out of 15 initiatives on this subject had been passed and only 3 rejected.
- **Secret ballots for labour (trade) union elections:** approved in Arizona, South Carolina and Utah.
- **Banning affirmative action programmes:** Arizona voters approved Proposition 107 that prohibited the state from discriminating for or against individuals on the basis of race or ethnicity, effectively banning any form of affirmative action. States which had previously passed similar measures are California, Michigan, Nebraska and Washington.
- **Greenhouse gases:** California voters rejected Proposition 23, an initiative sponsored by two Texas oil companies, which would have suspended — until the economy improved — a state law passed in 2006 requiring reductions in

greenhouse gas emissions. Opposition from the outgoing governor and both gubernatorial candidates turned the tide on this one, leading to a 39%–61% defeat.

- **State name change proposal:** voters in the state of Rhode Island rejected an initiative that would have changed the name of their state from 'Rhode Island and the Providence Plantations' to simply 'Rhode Island'. Supporters of the measure had argued that the reference to plantations in the state's official name evoked memories of the state's slaveholding past.
- **Animal rights:** voters in Missouri approved Proposition B that establishes minimum space requirements for dog breeders, but North Dakota voters rejected an initiative that would have banned hunting in fenced game reserves. Voters in Arkansas, South Carolina and Tennessee approved constitutional amendments guaranteeing residents of their states a right to hunt and fish, but voters in Arizona rejected a similar measure.

What about 2011?

Most states don't hold state-wide elections in odd-numbered years; they hold them only in those years when there are congressional races. So the number of state-wide ballot measures in 2011 was far smaller than the 160 of 2010. There were just 34 state-wide ballot measures involving nine states in 2011.

The two high-profile measures came in Ohio. A proposed amendment to the state constitution to forbid any person or business from being compelled to participate in a healthcare system — as mandated by Obama's 2010 healthcare reforms — was passed overwhelmingly, by 66% to 34%. But voters rejected a law passed by the Ohio state legislature which limited collective bargaining for public employees by a similarly wide margin — 39% to 61%. The first result will please Republicans; the second will please Democrats. No wonder they call Ohio a 'swing' state.

Recall madness

As of the start of 2011, in all of American history, just 20 efforts to recall state legislators had gathered enough signatures to trigger a recall election. Thirteen of those 20 elections resulted in the successful recall of the state legislator. So when the state of Wisconsin held elections to recall nine of its state legislators in 2011, one could have been forgiven for thinking things had got a little out of hand. This spate of recall elections was the result of the fracas surrounding Republican Governor Scott Walker's budget repair bill which included significant limitations on the collective bargaining rights of public employee unions. In order to try to stop a vote on the legislation, all 14 of the Democrat state senators 'fled' across the state line to Illinois, hoping thereby to prevent the presence of a quorum in the state senate, and consequently prevent a vote. Republican activists in Wisconsin then started recall proceedings against six of the state senate Democrats alleging that they had 'failed to turn up for work'.

Democrat activists retaliated by starting recall proceedings against three of the state senate Republicans, alleging that they were not representing their constituents by supporting the governor's budget bill.

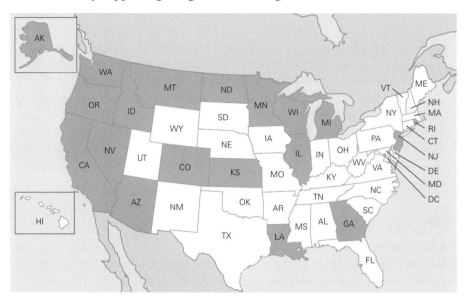

Figure 5.5 States with provision for recall of state officials

First up was Democrat State Senator Dave Hansen who survived his recall election on 19 July, winning 67% of the vote. Then on 9 August, six Republican state senators were up for recall. Four won, but two — Dan Kapanke and Randy Hopper — were defeated by their Democrat opponents. Kapanke lost by 10 percentage points; Hopper by just 2. On 16 August, two more Democrat state senators faced a recall but both comfortably survived the challenge — Robert Birch with 58% of the vote and Jim Holperin with 55%.

Questions

1 How many initiatives were voted on in 2010 and what percentage of them were approved?
2 What do the states which make most use of initiatives have in common geographically?
3 Why did the results of initiatives in 2010 favour a conservative position?
4 Give three examples of 2010 initiatives.
5 What happened regarding state-wide ballot measures in 2011?
6 (a) What triggered the nine recall elections in Wisconsin in 2011? (b) What were the results of these elections?

Chapter 6

Rights to the right?

What you need to know

- **Civil rights** are positive acts of government designed to protect persons against arbitrary or discriminatory treatment by government or individuals.
- **Civil liberties** are those liberties, mostly spelled out in the Constitution, that guarantee the protection of persons, expression and property from arbitrary interference by the government.
- The **Bill of Rights** is the first ten amendments to the Constitution added in 1791.

Does everyone in the USA possess the same rights? That's a complicated question to answer. Do all similar people possess the same rights? For example, do all women have the same rights? Do all men have the same rights? Do all immigrants have the same rights? We tend to presume that the answer to these questions is 'yes', the reason being because they live under the same federal laws, the same Supreme Court decisions and the same Constitution.

What about state variations? Do people in the state of Minnesota have the same rights as people in the state of New York? Clearly they do not with regard to some rights. New York has just passed a state law permitting same-sex 'marriage', whereas Minnesota is preparing for a state-wide vote in 2012 which would define marriage as a union between 'one man and one woman'. And although all women in the USA might presume they have the same abortion rights — courtesy of the Supreme Court's *Roe* v *Wade* decision in 1973 — some states are now introducing laws which significantly limit that right. New York's move to approve gay 'marriage' is something of an exception, being a liberalisation of rights. Most moves on the civil rights front have been to the right — in a more conservative direction — not to the left. So in what ways and where are rights and liberties moving to the right?

Abortion rights

Perhaps the most remarkable rightward shift in 2011 has come in the area of abortion rights for women. Fifteen states (Figure 6.1) have reduced the availability of abortions within their borders during the past year. Thirteen of these 15 are states which voted Republican in four or all five of the past five presidential elections. Only one state — Wisconsin — has voted Democrat in all the last five presidential elections. The other — Florida — has voted three times for the Republican and twice for the Democrat candidate. But essentially, these are what we call 'red' — that is conservative, Republican

— states. Little surprise, therefore that they have moved in a conservative direction on the matter of abortion.

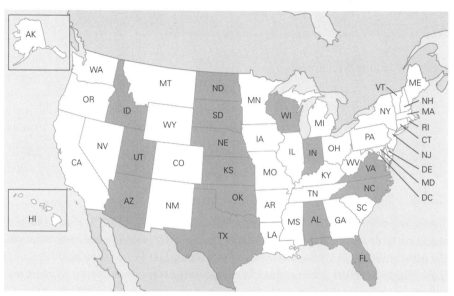

Figure 6.1 States which limited abortion rights in 2011

Table 6.1 Changes in abortion rights by state

| State | Conservative | | | | |
	Mandatory ultrasound	Waiting period and counselling	Limit on insurance coverage	20-week ban	Defund Planned Parenthood
Alabama				●	
Arizona	●				
Florida	●		●		
Idaho			●	●	
Indiana	●	●	●	●	●
Kansas	●	●	●	●	●
Nebraska			●		
North Carolina			●		●
North Dakota		●			
Oklahoma			●	●	
South Dakota		●			
Texas	●	●			
Utah			●		
Virginia			●		
Wisconsin					●

Source: *National Journal*, 23 July 2011, p. 20

But how have they limited the availability of abortion? The details are shown in Table 6.1. Five states have approved legislation requiring women wishing to have an abortion to first receive an ultrasound examination. Another five states have extended the waiting period for women who request an abortion. South Dakota has extended the period from 24 to 72 hours — the longest waiting period in the nation. Indiana now requires that women undergo counselling on the pain likely to be suffered by the foetus and, along with Kansas, insists that medical staff tell women that foetuses are 'people'. Nine states have imposed restrictions on insurance funding for abortion. Five states have banned abortions after 20 weeks of conception. Four states have removed state funding from Planned Parenthood, a group that provides health services including abortion. Indiana and Kansas have put all five of these restrictions in place.

Guns

'Opponents of gun control gained as much ground in 2011 as anti-abortion activists have,' claimed Ronald Brownstein in a cover story article in *National Journal* in July 2011 ('Separate ways', 23 July 2011). Fourteen states expanded gun rights in 2011 — that is moved ideologically to the right in this area (Figure 6.2). Seven of those 14 were states which had moved in the same direction on abortion.

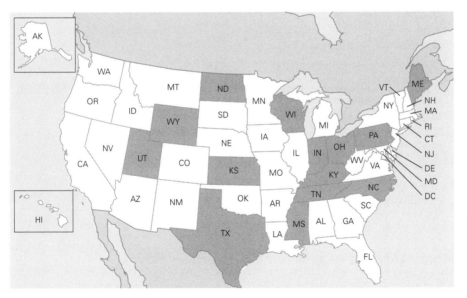

Figure 6.2 States which expanded gun rights in 2011

The laws expanding gun rights in these 14 states varied in scope and nature. North Carolina and Pennsylvania both passed stronger so-called 'castle laws' — that is laws allowing citizens to defend themselves in their homes with deadly force. The other 12 states expanded gun rights by relaxing carrying restrictions. So, for example, North Dakota and Texas passed laws in 2011 allowing people to keep weapons in a car left unattended in a car park. Wisconsin legislated to allow the carrying of concealed weapons.

Again, these 'right turns' on rights came mainly in red states. Ten of the 14 states that lightened restrictions on gun possession voted Republican in at least three of the last five presidential elections — the only exceptions being Maine, Ohio, Pennsylvania and Wisconsin.

Whereas there was no move to the 'left' on abortion in any state in 2011, there was one state which moved in the liberal direction on guns. In Maryland — a state which has voted Democrat in all of the last five presidential elections — the state legislature passed a law in 2011 which required stronger punishments for repeat-offender gun-related crimes. But this was the only state to move to the left on gun rights (Table 6.2).

Table 6.2 Changes in gun rights by state

| State | Liberal | Conservative | |
	Stronger gun crime penalties	Stronger 'castle laws'	Lighter carry restrictions
Indiana			●
Kansas			●
Kentucky			●
Maine			●
Maryland	●		
Mississippi			●
North Carolina		●	●
North Dakota			●
Ohio			●
Pennsylvania		●	
Tennessee			●
Texas			●
Utah			●
Wisconsin			●
Wyoming			●

Source: *National Journal*, 23 July 2011, p. 23

More rightward — and some leftward — moves

Abortion and guns were not the only areas to see a rightward move on rights in 2011. Thirteen states passed laws to limit the bargaining rights of public-employee unions. Eight of these states had Republican governors and Republican-controlled state legislatures. Of the remaining five, only one did not have a Republican governor.

Immigration was another area to see some significant changes in state law — another area in which the federal government has failed to pass any meaningful reform of late. Here 14 states moved in a more conservative direction with just five moving in a more liberal direction. In the conservative column, five states passed immigration-enforcement laws similar to the controversial law passed in Arizona in 2010, and seven states adopted laws requiring voters to show photo identification to vote, in an attempt to cut down on voting by illegal immigrants. By contrast, Democrat governors in five other states — all with Republican-controlled legislatures — vetoed voter-ID legislation.

The only rights area which saw a significant leftward movement in 2011 was that of gay rights. Four states — Delaware, Hawaii, Illinois and Rhode Island (all strongly Democratic states) — passed civil partnership laws for gay couples. And on 24 June 2011, New York became the sixth, and by far the largest, state to legalise gay 'marriage'.

Conclusion

So we can see clearly that not all Americans do have the same rights. But does this variation in rights across the 50 states actually matter? Here's Ronald Brownstein again:

> There's nothing new about states charting distinct pathways. Many thinkers have long championed the idea of states as 'laboratories of democracy' that provide a testing ground for competing ideas. But this year's flurry of legislative activity is testing the limits of that theory dramatically, widening the gap between policies in blue and red states on polarising issues such as abortion, gay rights and immigration.

What we see here, therefore, is more of the ideological and partisan polarisation that defines contemporary Washington politics increasingly appearing in the debates and law-making decisions in the state capitals as well.

Questions
1 How many states reduced the availability of abortions in 2011?
2 What do 13 of these states have in common?
3 Analyse and explain the data shown in Table 6.1.
4 How many states expanded gun rights in 2011?
5 What are 'castle laws'?
6 In what other ways did some states expand gun rights in 2011?
7 In what other policy areas was a rightward shift in rights and liberties seen in some states in 2011?
8 Explain the quotation from Ronald Brownstein.

The Supreme Court, 2010–11

What you need to know

- The Supreme Court is the highest federal court in the USA.
- The Court is made up of nine justices, appointed by the president, for life.
- Of the nine justices who served in the term we consider in this chapter, five were appointed by Republican presidents and four by Democrats.
- The Supreme Court has the power of judicial review. This is the power to declare acts of Congress or actions of the executive branch — or acts or actions of state governments — unconstitutional, and thereby null and void.
- By this power of judicial review, the Court acts as the umpire of the Constitution and plays a leading role in safeguarding Americans' rights and liberties.

The 2010–11 term was the second in succession in which a new justice served her first term. The 2009–10 term was the first term for President Obama's first Supreme Court nominee, Sonia Sotomayor. The 2010–11 term was the first term for his second nominee, Elena Kagan. So Court-watchers were looking to see if both Justice Sotomayor and Justice Kagan were making judgements as expected or whether either was showing any trend in a different direction. Both were presumed to be liberal — or 'loose constructionist' — justices. Both replaced similarly liberal justices, respectively David Souter and John Paul Stevens.

Some Supreme Court terms go down in history for producing blockbuster, landmark decisions. The 2009–10 brought one such decision in *Citizens United* v *Federal Election Commission*, a 1st Amendment freedom of speech case. But the 2010–11 term brought no such notable judgements. It might be the calm before the storm, with the 2011–12 expected to bring the Court's decision on Arizona's immigration law and Obama's healthcare reform. However, that's not to say that there was nothing of interest during this most recent term. There are three cases worthy of study, all of them invoking the 1st Amendment (Table 7.1).

Table 7.1 Significant Supreme Court decisions, 2010–11 term

Case	Concerning	Decision
Snyder v *Phelps*	Protests at military funerals	8–1
Brown v *Entertainment Merchants Association*	Sale of violent video games to minors	7–2
Arizona Free Enterprise v *Bennett*	Campaign finance regulation	5–4

Hateful speech at military funerals

The decision which provoked the most public comment was that of *Snyder* v *Phelps* in which the Court upheld, by 8 votes to 1, the right of a fringe church to stage anti-gay protests at military funerals. The case arose from an anti-gay protest staged in 2006 by members of the tiny, family-run, Westboro Baptist Church in Topeka, Kansas, at the funeral of 20-year old Matthew Snyder in Westminster, Maryland. Snyder had been killed in Iraq and his was one of more than 600 funerals picketed by the Reverend Fred Phelps and members of his family, including his daughter Margie Phelps. Matthew Snyder's father took out the lawsuit against Phelps saying the group had turned his son's funeral into a 'circus'. The group, which believes that God is punishing the USA for its tolerance of homosexuality, had held up signs and chanted slogans such as 'Thank God for dead soldiers', 'God hates fags' and 'America is doomed'. (It should be noted that Matthew Snyder was not gay.)

But the Court's most liberal and most conservative members joined together in the 8–1 decision, authored by Chief Justice John Roberts. In his majority opinion, the chief justice stated:

> While these messages may fall short of refined social or political commentary, the issues they highlight — the political and moral conduct of the United States and its citizens, the fate of our nation, homosexuality in the military, and scandals involving the Catholic clergy — are matters of public importance.

But to Roberts and his seven colleagues, the 1st Amendment right to freedom of speech had to take precedence over causing distress at a family funeral — and distressing it undoubtedly was. Roberts went on to conclude:

> Speech is powerful. It can stir people to action, move them to tears of both joy and sorrow, and — as it did here — inflict great pain. On the facts before us, we cannot react to that pain by punishing the speaker. As a Nation we have chosen a different course — to protect even hurtful speech on public issues to ensure that we do not stifle public debate.

In an amicus curiae brief to the Court, the Reporters Committee for Freedom of the Press and 21 news organisations, including the New York Times Company, supported the rights of Westboro Baptist Church. 'To silence a fringe messenger because of the distastefulness of the message,' the brief stated, 'is antithetical to the 1st Amendment's most basic precepts.'

This was all too much for the lone dissenter in this case, Justice Samuel Alito, who said his colleagues were wrong. In his dissent, he said the Constitution's guarantee of free speech in the 1st Amendment did not allow folk from Westboro Baptist Church to 'brutalise' the Snyder family with their lewd and cruel messages. In Alito's view, the Snyder family had rights too — to bury their son in peace — and the protesters had no right to launch what Alito called 'a malevolent verbal attack on Matthew and his family at a time of acute emotional vulnerability'. Alito concluded:

> Our profound national commitment to free and open debate is not a licence for the vicious verbal assault that occurred in this case.

Alito's dissent in this case shows that he is a justice who is willing to strike out on his own, even when his fellow conservatives — Roberts, Scalia and Thomas — go in a different direction.

Violent video games being sold to children

In another 1st Amendment case, *Brown* v *Entertainment Merchants Association*, the Court — by a margin of 7 votes to 2 — declared a California state law banning the sale of violent video games to children unconstitutional. In his majority opinion, Justice Antonin Scalia stated that:

> Like the protected books, plays and movies that preceded them, video games communicate ideas — and even social messages — through many familiar devices (such as characters, dialogue, plot and music) and through features distinctive to the medium (such as the player's interaction with the virtual world).

All this, in Scalia's view, 'suffices to confer 1st Amendment protection'. Addressing the issue of violence, Scalia again used the parallel of more traditional children's entertainment stating that '*Grimm's Fairy Tales*, for example, are grim indeed', and then going on to recount the gory plots of such childhood favourites as *Snow White*, *Cinderella* and *Hansel and Gretel*, not to mention the repeated scenes of violence in *Tom and Jerry* cartoons. Justice Scalia agreed that some of the images in the games were both disturbing and disgusting, 'but disgust is not a valid basis for restricting expression', he wrote in a conclusion highly reminiscent of the *Snyder* decision.

Justice Scalia and his six colleagues also argued that the wording of the California statute was far too vague using, as it did, phrases such as 'patently offensive' and that which appealed to children's 'deviant or morbid interests'. Scalia was joined in whole by justices Anthony Kennedy, Ruth Bader Ginsburg, Sonia Sotomayor and Elena Kagan, and in part by Chief Justice Roberts and Justice Alito.

The two dissenting justices wrote separate opinions. Justice Thomas dissented as he did not believe the drafters of the 1st Amendment meant it to protect children's free speech rights. Justice Breyer dissented as he believed the California law was constitutional.

Campaign finance regulation

The case of *Arizona Free Enterprise* v *Bennett* was the Court's first campaign finance decision since its landmark *Citizens United* case in 2010. In this 2011 decision, the Court struck down Arizona's Clean Elections Act that provided extra matching funds (i.e. money from the government) to candidates who agreed to spend no more than $500 of their own money, participate in at least one public debate and return any unspent money. Lawyers defending the Arizona law — a number of other states had similar laws — did so on the basis that it combats corruption, a defence with which they hoped the Court would agree. But at the oral argument stage back in March, Chief Justice Roberts questioned the defence lawyers on this, suggesting that it was not about cutting corruption but rather creating a level playing field among candidates, something which would be seen as contrary to 1st Amendment rights. Lawyers for Arizona argued that the purpose was not to 'level the playing field' by equalising candidates' resources. But Chief Justice Roberts had done his homework:

> Well, I checked the Citizens Clean Elections Commission website this morning, and it says that this act was passed to 'level the playing field' when it comes to running for office.

As George Will commented in the *Washington Post* ('A Supreme Court win for political speech and political money', 29 June 2011): 'Game over!'. Writing the majority opinion in this 5–4 decision, Roberts concluded that the government can still use taxpayer funds to subsidise political campaigns, but it can only do that in a manner that provides an alternative to private financing. It cannot create disincentives, as the Arizona law had done, and therefore was seen as regulating speech, in contravention of the 1st Amendment. Roberts was joined in the majority by fellow conservatives Scalia, Thomas and Alito, as well as by Justice Kennedy.

Court statistics

In the 2010–11 term, the Court delivered 80 opinions, slightly down on its unusually high figure of 86 in the previous term. This, however, continues to indicate a steady increase since Roberts succeeded William Rehnquist as chief justice in 2005. Of these 80 opinions, just 16 (20%) were 5–4 decisions, almost identical with the previous term (Table 7.2). However, these 5–4 decisions once again showed the ideological divide within the Court very clearly. In 14 of these 16 decisions (88%), all four members of the Court's conservative wing (Roberts, Scalia, Thomas and Alito) were on one side and all four of the Court's liberal wing (Ginsburg, Breyer, Sotomayor and Kagan) were on the other. Between them was Justice Kennedy. He joined the conservative quartet in ten (63%) of those 14 decisions giving them the majority and the liberal quartet in four (25%) decisions giving them the majority (Figure 7.1).

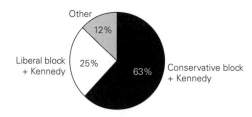

Figure 7.1 Composition of 5–4 majorities in 2010–11 term

Source: **www.scotusblog.com**

Table 7.2 Supreme Court statistics, 2005–11

	2005–06	2006–07	2007–08	2008–09	2009–10	2010–11
Number of opinions	69	68	67	74	86	80
Decided by 5–4	23%	35%	17%	31%	19%	20%
Justice(s) most in majority in 5–4 decisions	Kennedy	Kennedy	Kennedy Thomas	Kennedy	Kennedy Thomas Scalia	Kenned
Justice(s) most in minority in 5–4 decisions	Breyer	Stevens	Breyer	Breyer	Ginsburg	Breyer
% which conservatives won 5–4 decisions	55%	54%	33%	48%	50%	63%
% which liberals won 5–4 decisions	36%	25%	33%	22%	19%	25%
Two justices most in agreement	Roberts Alito	Roberts Alito	Roberts Scalia	Roberts Alito	Ginsburg Sotomayor	Roberts Alito
Two justices most in disagreement	Alito Stevens	Thomas Stevens	Thomas Stevens	Thomas Stevens	Thomas Stevens	Alito Ginsbur
Justice(s) most frequently in the majority	Roberts	Kennedy	Roberts	Kennedy	Roberts Kennedy	Kenned
Justice most frequently in the minority	Stevens	Stevens	Thomas	Stevens	Stevens	Ginsbur

The two justices most frequently in agreement were the two George W. Bush appointees — John Roberts and Samuel Alito — although they split on one of the three significant decisions of the term, that of *Snyder* v *Phelps*. The two justices agreed in 96% of the decisions of this term. But they were closely followed by the two Obama appointees — Sotomayor and Kagan — who agreed in 94% of cases. The two justices most at odds with one another were Alito and Ginsburg, who disagreed in 38% of the decisions. If one discounts the unanimous decisions of the Court, then Alito and Ginsburg were on different sides in 71% of cases.

The distinction for the justice most frequently in the majority during this term was Anthony Kennedy. He had shared the distinction with Chief Justice Roberts in the previous term and this is the third term in the last five that he has held this position on his own. In the 2009–10 term, Kennedy was in the majority in 94% of cases, followed by Roberts (91%), Thomas (88%) and both

Scalia and Alito (86%). Furthermore, when it came to the 5–4 decisions, the conservative quartet of Roberts, Scalia, Thomas and Alito, joined by Kennedy, won in 63% of them. This is the highest percentage for the conservatives in over 10 years. So the conservatives yet again dominated the Court in this term. The justice most frequently in the minority was Justice Ginsburg — a position taken in 8 of the last 11 terms by recently retired justice John Paul Stevens.

Kagan's first term

How did Elena Kagan fair in her first term on the high court? Her prior service as solicitor general in the Obama administration required her to not participate in one-third of this term's cases. But despite that, she made quite an impressive start to her Supreme Court career:

- She voted as one might have expected: voting most often with liberal justices Sotomayor (94%), Ginsburg (90%) and Breyer (88%).
- The justice with whom she agreed least was Clarence Thomas (65%, and only 38% in non-unanimous cases).
- She wrote seven majority opinions during her first term — the same as Justice Alito wrote in his first term in 2006.
- The average number of days she took to write her opinions from the day of oral argument to announcing the opinion was 96 days, making her the fourth quickest worker on the Court. (Sotomayor was the quickest, averaging 84 days; Kennedy the slowest at 127 days.)
- Linda Greenhouse in the *New York Times* ('A Supreme Court scorecard', 13 July 2011) stated that despite having no previous judicial experience, Kagan asked searching questions and wrote 'full-throated' opinions.

Some justices are more talkative than others

Since the arrival of Sotomayor (2009) and Kagan (2010), more questions are being asked at the oral argument stage. 'Supreme Court justices are talking more' was the headline of a *Washington Post* article by Robert Barnes (1 March 2011). Talking of the current justices, Lisa Blatt, who has argued before the Court on a number of occasions, stated:

> They're way more active than they've ever been. They ask a lot more questions. As active as [former] Justice Souter was, Justice Sotomayor [who replaced him] is more active. And as active as [former] Justice Stevens was, Justice Kagan [who replaced him] is more active than that.

The chatty Justice Kagan and the silent Justice Thomas display two quite different views of oral arguments. Speaking on CNN just after she joined the Court, Kagan had this to say:

> [The oral argument stage] is for us to say [to the lawyers], 'Well, yes, we've read your brief, we know what you think of the case, but here are the questions that that inspired in us.

Justice Thomas, who has asked no questions from the bench during the last 5 years, speaking on the same CNN programme, saw things differently:

> I think [the oral argument] is an opportunity for the lawyers to fill in the blanks, to make their case. I think you should allow people to complete their answers and their thought, and to continue their conversation. I find that far more helpful than the rapid-fire questions [from justices].

The following statistics tell us more about the way in which the justices see and play their role at oral arguments:

- Justice who on average asks the most questions at oral argument: Scalia: 25.
- Justice who on average asks the least questions at oral argument: Thomas: 0.
- Justice most likely to ask the first question at oral argument: Ginsburg: in 27% of cases, followed by Scalia (26%), Roberts (16%) and Sotomayor (13%).
- Justice who talks the most (as measured by lines of text in Court transcripts): Breyer, followed by Scalia and Sotomayor.

Looking ahead

Following a period of unparalleled stability with no change in its membership between 1994 and 2005, the Court has been through a period of change with four new justices — including the chief justice — joining the Court between 2005 and 2010. So what of the future?

As Table 7.3 shows, the four oldest members of the Court at the time of writing are Ginsburg (78), Scalia and Kennedy (both 75), and Breyer (73). Thomas, the fifth in line by age, is only 63. Thus if one were looking for an upcoming vacancy, Ginsburg has to be the most likely. She has also not been in good health of late. Ginsburg is probably now the most reliably liberal justice on the Court, following the retirement in 2010 of Justice Stevens. So if Obama were to name her replacement, he would likely replace one liberal with another — not a Court changer.

Table 7.3 Supreme Court justices ranked by age

Justice	Appointed by	Sworn in	Age on 1/1/2012
Ruth Bader Ginsburg	Clinton	1993	78
Antonin Scalia	Reagan	1986	75
Anthony Kennedy	Reagan	1988	75
Stephen Breyer	Clinton	1994	73
Clarence Thomas	George H. W. Bush	1991	63
Samuel Alito	George W. Bush	2006	61
Sonia Sotomayor	Obama	2009	57
John Roberts	George W. Bush	2005	56
Elena Kagan	Obama	2010	51

Meanwhile, the Court in its current make-up will probably continue to cut a path well to the right of the Obama administration, with many cases being decided by the conservative quartet of Roberts, Scalia, Thomas and Alito, joined by Justice Kennedy. And that 'quartet plus one' seems determined, from this term at least, to make the 1st Amendment their principle judicial platform.

As for the 2011–12 term which opened on Monday 3 October, this could be quite interesting. Speaking the weekend before the Court term opened, Paul Clement, solicitor general in the George W. Bush administration, stated: 'Whatever the last term lacked in blockbuster cases, here's one that's really for the ages.' Here are three cases to watch out for which are likely to be decided during 2012:

- *Florida* v *Department of Health and Human Services*. Does the Constitution's Commerce Clause (Article I, Section 8, Clause 3) give Congress the power to require Americans to obtain health insurance? This is a cornerstone provision of President Obama's 2010 healthcare legislation. A ruling in the case is likely in June 2012, right in the middle of the presidential election campaign. Were the Court to strike down the law, this would be a huge political blow for the President.
- *Federal Communications Commission* v *Fox Television Stations Inc.* Are the Federal Communications Commission's standards for indecency on television too vague? Another 1st Amendment case.
- *United States* v *Jones*. Do police need a warrant before attaching a global positioning system device to a person's car to track them 24 hours a day for a long period of time? The case is brought by a convicted Washington DC drug dealer.

Questions

1 Summarise the opposing views of Chief Justice Roberts and Justice Alito in the *Snyder* v *Phelps* decision.
2 Why did the Court declare a California state law banning the sale of violent video games to children unconstitutional?
3 Explain the Court's decision in *Arizona Free Enterprise* v *Bennett*.
4 What does Figure 7.1 tell us about the Court in 2010–11?
5 Analyse the data presented in the far right-hand column in Table 7.2.
6 How did Justice Kagan perform in her first term on the Supreme Court?
7 What prospect does President Obama have of being able to change the ideological make-up of the Supreme Court?
8 What important cases are likely to be decided by the Court in 2012?

Chapter 8

Is the US Constitution past its use-by date?

What you need to know

- The US Constitution is made up of seven articles and 27 amendments.
- The seven articles were drawn up at the constitutional convention in Philadelphia in 1787.
- The first ten amendments, known collectively as the Bill of Rights, were added in 1791.
- Constitutional amendments can be proposed either by Congress (with two-thirds majorities in both houses) or by a national constitutional convention (the latter has never been used).
- Amendments must then be ratified either by three-quarters of the state legislatures or by three-quarters of the states in state constitutional conventions.

It is now 225 years since the Founding Fathers gathered in Philadelphia in the summer of 1787 and drew up in essence what we know today as the US Constitution. Of the 18 pages that the Constitution takes up at the back of one A-level textbook, 10 pages are taken by the original seven articles, while the 27 amendments take up the remaining 8 pages. Box 8.1 shows some of the more significant amendments added in the last 150 years. But is a document written largely two-and-a-quarter centuries ago now past its use-by date? Is a (largely) eighteenth century document workable in the twenty-first century?

Box 8.1   Selected constitutional amendments since 1865

- Slavery ended (13th, 1865)
- Federal income tax permitted (16th, 1913)
- Senate directly elected (17th, 1913)
- Women given the vote (19th, 1920)
- Presidential terms limited (22nd, 1951)
- Voting age lowered to 18 (26th, 1971)

Does the Constitution still work?

Gerald Ford, the 38th president, addressed the American people on 9 August 1974 immediately after having become president following the resignation of President Nixon over the Watergate affair. In this memorable speech, Ford declared:

My fellow Americans, our long national nightmare is over. Our Constitution works.

Richard Nixon probably did not appreciate being described as 'a long national nightmare', so we'll pass over the first sentence, but what of Ford's claim that the 'Constitution works'? Was he right? Like all good questions, this provokes both a 'yes' and a 'no' answer. We'll take the 'no' answer first. There are certain parts of the Constitution for which you can make out a strong case that it does not work any more — that it is well past its use-by date. We shall consider four examples.

War-making powers

There are three sections of the Constitution which have something to say about war-making powers: one concerns the president; the other two concern the Congress. Article II Section 2 states that:

> The President shall be Commander in Chief of the armed forces.

It actually says 'Army and Navy', but 'armed forces' is the more appropriate modern-day phrase. Article I Section 8 states that:

> Congress shall have the Power to declare war.

Furthermore, Article I Section 9 states that:

> No money shall be drawn from the Treasury, but in consequence of appropriations made by law.

It is this latter provision which we refer to as Congress's 'power of the purse'.

These three provisions of the Constitution are meant to provide one of the many checks and balances between the president and Congress. Congress's power to declare war and to approve all spending bills is meant to check the president's power as commander-in-chief. But it simply no longer works. Congress has declared war only five times, the most recent occasion being 1941 following the Japanese attack on Pearl Harbour. Yet Box 8.2 shows that since then, the US military has been in almost constant use in overseas conflicts. Indeed, during the last 60 years there have been only 19 calendar years when US troops have not been involved in foreign hostilities, and the longest period of 'peace' was a mere 6 years between 1976 and 1982.

| **Box 8.2** | **Use of troops abroad since last declaration of war** |

- Korea (1950–53)
- Vietnam (1960–75)
- Cuba (1961)
- Grenada (1983)
- Panama (1989)
- Persian Gulf (1990–91)
- Bosnia and Herzegovina (1995–96)
- Afghanistan (2001–)
- Iraq (2003–)
- Libya (2011–)

As for Congress's power of the purse, the severe limitations of this power were shown during the 2003–09 period of the George W. Bush presidency, when both Republican-controlled (2003–06) and Democrat-controlled (2007–09) Congresses proved unwilling or unable to exercise much control over presidential foreign policy through the budgetary process. And this is no new problem. Back in February 1983, Republican president Reagan's secretary of defense, Caspar Weinberger, was appearing before the Democrat-controlled Senate Budget Committee. During the hearing, Democrat Senator Donald Riegle of Michigan had this to say to Secretary Weinberger:

> I think that *your* overspending on defence is distorting the economy, bloating the deficits, adding to unemployment, keeping interest rates at excessively high levels. *You* are mortgaging our future with enormous increases in the national debt. [Emphasis added]

Eventually allowed to reply to these and other accusations, Secretary Weinberger asked the senator:

> I wonder if you can tell me how *I* can spend one nickel of defence money that has not been appropriated by the Congress — by you and your colleagues? The Congress thus far has authorised all the amounts of money we are spending. To say that *I* am spending the country into bankruptcy is to say the Congress has authorised too much. I do not think they have. [Emphasis added]

Game, set and match to Mr Weinberger! Senator Riegle seemed to have temporarily forgotten his Constitution, but one can sympathise with the senator's frustrations. The power of the purse is rarely all it's made out to be, especially in the field of national security and defence policy.

Supreme Court confirmations

Article II Section 2 of the Constitution states that:

> The President shall nominate and, by and with the Advice and Consent of the Senate, shall appoint judges of the Supreme Court.

The issue here is the way the Senate now plays its 'advice and consent' role. Time was when the Senate made this decision based solely on judicial qualification — in other words, was the nominee of the highest calibre to be regarded as one of top nine jurists in the USA? The hearings on the nominee were conducted in a highly professional manner, and voting, where it took place at all, was bipartisan. The process was cordial and quick.

Back in 1975, John Paul Stevens was nominated by President Ford to a vacancy on the Court caused by the retirement of William Douglas. Despite the fact that Ford was a Republican, that the Democrats had a significant majority in the Senate, and that Stevens — regarded at the time as a centrist/conservative judge — was to replace 'the most committed civil libertarian ever to sit on the Court', Stevens was confirmed by the Senate 98–0. From Ford's announcement to the Senate's confirmation took just 19 days.

In 2010, Elena Kagan was nominated by President Obama to the Court to fill the vacancy caused by Stevens' retirement. Despite the fact that Obama was a Democrat, the Democrats held a comfortable majority in the Senate, and that Kagan — regarded as a liberal judge — was to replace Stevens who was by the end of his tenure the most reliably liberal member of the Court, Kagan was confirmed but received the votes of only 5 Republican senators in her 63–37 tally. From Obama's announcement to the Senate's confirmation had taken 87 days.

Tables 8.1 and 8.2 show how things have changed both in terms of the increase in the length of time the confirmation process takes and the decrease in the level of bipartisanship. Things changed significantly after the hearings in 1987 over the nomination by President Reagan of Robert Bork. Bork was rejected after a highly politicised and angry confirmation process. Things got even worse in 1991 at the hearings into the nomination by President George H. W. Bush of Clarence Thomas. Thomas himself described the Senate confirmation process as 'a circus, a national disgrace, a high-tech lynching'.

Table 8.1 Days from nomination to confirmation of Supreme Court justices, 1975–2010

Justice	Nominated by	Year	Days from nomination to confirmation
John Paul Stevens	Gerald Ford	1975	19
Sandra O'Connor	Ronald Reagan	1981	33
Antonin Scalia	Ronald Reagan	1986	85
Anthony Kennedy	Ronald Reagan	1988	65
David Souter	George H. W. Bush	1990	69
Clarence Thomas	George H. W. Bush	1991	99
Ruth Bader Ginsburg	Bill Clinton	1993	50
Stephen Breyer	Bill Clinton	1994	73
John Roberts	George W. Bush	2005	23
Samuel Alito	George W. Bush	2006	82
Sonia Sotomayor	Barack Obama	2009	66
Elena Kagan	Barack Obama	2010	87

Table 8.2 'Yes' votes by opposition party senators on Supreme Court nominees, 1990–2010

Nominee	Date	President/party	'Yes' votes by opposition party senators
David Souter	1990	Bush (R)	D: 46
Clarence Thomas	1991	Bush (R)	D: 11
Ruth Bader Ginsburg	1993	Clinton (D)	R: 41
Stephen Breyer	1994	Clinton (D)	R: 33
John Roberts	2005	Bush (R)	D: 22
Samuel Alito	2006	Bush (R)	D: 4
Sonia Sotomayor	2009	Obama (D)	R: 9
Elena Kagan	2010	Obama (D)	R: 5

In today's confirmation hearings, senators from the president's party now spend the time lobbing 'soft ball' questions at the nominee while those from the opposition party try to embarrass the nominee with questions that concentrate more on trivia and gossip than on judicial qualifications. Here's Republican senator Charles Grassley of Iowa questioning Judge Samuel Alito in 2006 — a nominee of Republican president George W. Bush:

> **GRASSLEY:** Judge Alito, do you believe that the executive branch should have unchecked authority?
>
> **ALITO:** Absolutely not, Senator.
>
> **GRASSLEY:** Judge Alito, do you understand that when constitutionally protected rights are involved, the courts have an important role to play in making sure that the executive branch does not trample those rights?
>
> **ALITO:** I certainly do, Senator.
>
> **GRASSLEY:** Do you believe that the president of the United States is above the law and the Constitution?
>
> **ALITO:** Nobody in this country is above the law, and that includes the president.

So Judge Alito believes in checks and balances, civil rights and equality before the law. Whatever next? Even a sixth grade civics student could answer these questions, the purpose of which is not to elicit information but just to make the nominee look good.

Meanwhile, the Democrats were busy trying to catch out Judge Alito — to make him out as some kind of bigot, or maybe a racist, or even a misogynist. 'Are you perhaps a closet bigot?' asked Republican senator Lindsay Graham of South Carolina, trying to embarrass his Democrat colleagues for asking what he doubtless regarded as tactless and embarrassing questions. And when it was all over, an editorial in the *Washington Post* summed it up thus:

> The hearings were less illuminating than might have been hoped. Democratic senators often seemed more interested in attacking the nominee — sometimes scurrilously — than in probing what sort of justice he would be. Republican senators, meanwhile, acted more as fatuous counsels for the defence than as sober evaluators of a nominee to serve on the Supreme Court. On both sides, pious, meandering speeches outnumbered thoughtful questions. As a result, Americans don't know all that much more about Judge Alito than they did before.

And when all was said and done, the Senate confirmed Judge Alito on what was virtually a party-line vote with all bar one Republican voting 'yes' and all bar four Democrats voting 'no'. It could certainly be argued that this provision of the Constitution is also past its use-by date.

The Electoral College

The 12th Amendment states that:

> The Electors shall meet in their respective states, and vote by ballot for
> President and Vice-President.

This 1804 provision replaced part of the detailed provision for the Electoral
College laid out in 1787 in Article II Section 1 of the Constitution. Clearly,
therefore, the Electoral College is a creation of more than two centuries ago
and is regarded by many as well past its use-by date:

- It is based on the principle of indirect — rather than direct — election.
- It over-represents the voice of the small population states.
- The winner-takes-all principle (used in 48 of the 50 states) distorts the result
  of the popular vote.
- It is grossly unfair to national third parties.
- So-called 'rogue' or 'faithless' electors can potentially sabotage the result.

Most seriously of all, it is possible for the presidential candidate who wins the
popular vote to lose in the Electoral College and thereby win the presidency.
This has occurred three times: in 1876, 1888 and 2000. In 2000, Democrat
Al Gore won 48.4% of the popular vote to Republican George W. Bush's
48.0% — half-a-million more people voted for Gore than Bush. But because
of the distortion of the Electoral College, Bush won in the Electoral College by
271 votes to 266. (Actually, Gore should have received 267 votes but a rogue
Elector in Washington DC abstained rather than vote for him.)

Following the 2000 fiasco, there were some minor rumblings about reform
but they passed quickly and almost unreported. The nearest Congress ever
came to abolishing the Electoral College was after the 1968 election, in which
Republican Richard Nixon had defeated Democrat Hubert Humphrey by
less than 1% of the popular vote but by 301 to 191 in the Electoral College.
Had Humphrey received another 512,000 votes, he would have won the
popular vote but could have lost in the Electoral College by over 100 votes.
In September 1969, with President Nixon's support, the House approved
a constitutional amendment to abolish the Electoral College by 339 votes
to 70 — well over the required two-thirds majority. But the proposal was
blocked by a filibuster in the Senate and the amendment failed — another
opportunity missed to bring the US Constitution into the modern era. The
Electoral College is another part of the Constitution which many regard as
well past its use-by date.

Guns

The 2nd Amendment states:

> A well regulated Militia, being necessary to the security of a free State, the
> right of the people to keep and bear Arms, shall not be infringed.

Supreme Court justices and constitutional experts can barely agree on what these 27 words actually mean. Did the framers mean to enshrine in the Constitution a *collective* right with the emphasis on the first and second clauses relating to the formation of state militias; or did they mean to enshrine an *individual right* with the emphasis on the third clause? The former view is the one taken by most liberals, Democrats and supporters of gun control legislation; the latter view is the one taken by most conservatives, Republicans and opponents of gun control legislation. Until recently, the US Supreme Court had never clearly ruled on which view was correct, but in *District of Columbia* v *Heller* in 2008, by a 5–4 majority, the Court agreed with the latter — the individualist — view. (For a detailed study of this case see *US Government & Politics: Annual Survey 2010*, pp. 18–20.)

The supporters of this view such as the National Rifle Association (NRA) tell us that 'Guns don't kill people; people kill people'. In other words, there is little or no connection between gun ownership and gun deaths. Let's test that hypothesis. In the UK, 4% of households own a gun and the number of gun deaths per 100,000 deaths is just over 1. In the USA, 39% of households own a gun and the number of gun deaths per 100,000 deaths is 9. So the NRA is telling us that the higher proportion of gun deaths in the USA has nothing to do with higher gun ownership? The 2nd Amendment was undoubtedly appropriate to the largely rural and scattered communities of the late eighteenth and early nineteenth centuries, but in 2012, it is surely well past its use-by date.

Conclusions

Thus we have claimed that four important provisions of the US Constitution are well past their use-by date: provisions relating to matters as varied as war-making, judicial appointments, presidential elections and gun ownership.

But in other important ways, the Constitution has been continually updated — not by formal amendment but by judicial interpretation. 'We are under a Constitution, but the Constitution is what the judges say it is,' famously remarked Chief Justice Charles Evans Hughes just over a century ago. Chief Justice Hughes was referring to the Court's power of judicial review by which it can interpret the Constitution — saying what the words of the eighteenth century mean today.

Numerous provisions of the Constitution have been updated through the Court's interpretation:
- the 'common defense and general welfare' clause of Article I, Section 8
- the 1st Amendment's provisions that 'Congress shall make no law respecting an establishment of religion…or abridging freedom of Speech'
- the 5th Amendment's provision that 'No person…shall be compelled to be a witness against himself'

- the 8th Amendment's ban on 'cruel and unusual punishments'
- the 14th Amendment's guaranteeing of 'life, liberty and property'

In such landmark decisions as *Engel* v *Vitale* (1962), *Texas* v *Johnson* (1989), *Furman* v *Georgia* (1972) and *Roe* v *Wade* (1973), the Court has tried to ensure that the Constitution has not gone past its use-by date. Whether or not the Court should perform such a role, of course, is entirely another matter. But it has, and does, and doubtless will continue to do so. So long as the Court continues to exercise this power, the Constitution will not be entirely outdated. In that sense, President Ford was probably more right than wrong to assert that the Constitution works.

Questions

1 What did President Ford say about the US Constitution in August 1974?
2 What constitutional problems have arisen regarding war-making powers?
3 What point was Caspar Weinberger making in his answer to Senator Riegle?
4 Analyse the data presented in Tables 8.1 and 8.2.
5 What other problems have arisen about the constitutional provisions for the confirmation of Supreme Court justices?
6 What point was the *Washington Post* editorial making regarding the confirmation hearings for Samuel Alito?
7 What constitutional problems have arisen regarding the Electoral College?
8 What problems have arisen concerning the 2nd Amendment?
9 In what ways has the US Constitution been updated other than by formal amendment?

Who's who in US politics 2012

Executive branch

President .... Barack Obama
Vice-President .... Joe Biden

The cabinet

Secretary of State .... Hillary Clinton
Secretary of Defense .... Leon Panetta
Secretary of the Treasury .... Timothy Geithner
Secretary of Agriculture .... Tom Vilsack
Secretary of the Interior .... Ken Salazar
Attorney General (Justice Department) ...... Eric Holder
Secretary of Commerce .... John Bryson
Secretary of Labor .... Hilda Solis
Secretary of Health and Human Services ... Kathleen Sebelius
Secretary of Education .... Arne Duncan
Secretary of Housing and Urban Development ... Shaun Donovan
Secretary of Transportation .... Ray LaHood
Secretary of Energy .... Steven Chu
Secretary of Veterans' Affairs .... Eric Shinseki
Secretary of Homeland Security .... Janet Napolitano

Executive Office of the President personnel

White House Chief of Staff .... William Daley
Director of Office of Management and Budget ... Jacob Lew
Chairman of Council of Economic Advisers ... Alan Krueger
Domestic Policy Council Director .... Melody Barnes
National Security Adviser .... Tom Donilon
Assistant to the President for Legislative Affairs ... Rob Nabors
Trade Representative .... Ron Kirk
Press Secretary .... Jay Carney

Other executive branch personnel

Director of Central Intelligence Agency (CIA)	David Petraeus
Director of Federal Bureau of Investigation (FBI)	Robert Mueller
Chairman of the Joint Chiefs of Staff (JCS)	General Martin Dempsey

Legislative branch

Senate leadership

President Pro Tempore of the Senate	Daniel Inouye (D–Hawaii)
Senate Majority Leader	Harry Reid (D–Nevada)
Senate Minority Leader	Mitch McConnell (R–Kentucky)
Senate Majority Whip	Dick Durbin (D–Illinois)
Senate Minority Whip	Jon Kyl (R–Arizona)

House leadership

Speaker of the House of Representatives	John Boehner (R–Ohio)
House Majority Leader	Eric Cantor (R–Virginia)
House Minority Leader	Nancy Pelosi (D–California)
House Majority Whip	Kevin McCarthy (R–California)
House Minority Whip	Steny Hoyer (D–Maryland)

Senate Standing Committee chairs

Agriculture, Nutrition and Forestry	Debbie Stabenow	Michigan
Appropriations	Daniel Inouye	Hawaii
Armed Services	Carl Levin	Michigan
Banking, Housing and Urban Affairs	Tim Johnson	South Dakota
Budget	Kent Conrad	North Dakota
Commerce, Science and Transportation	Jay Rockefeller	West Virginia
Energy and Natural Resources	Jeff Bingaman	New Mexico
Environment and Public Works	Barbara Boxer	California
Finance	Max Baucus	Montana
Foreign Relations	John Kerry	Massachusetts
Health, Education, Labor and Pensions	Tom Harkin	Iowa
Homeland Security and Governmental Affairs	Joseph Lieberman	Connecticut
Judiciary	Patrick Leahy	Vermont
Rules and Administration	Charles Schumer	New York
Small Business and Entrepreneurship	Mary Landrieu	Louisiana
Veterans' Affairs	Daniel Akaka	Hawaii

House Standing Committee chairs

Agriculture	Frank Lucas	Oklahoma
Appropriations	Harold Rogers	Kentucky
Armed Services	Howard McKeon	California
Budget	Paul Ryan	Wisconsin
Education and the Workforce	John Kline	Minnesota
Energy and Commerce	Fred Upton	Michigan
Financial Services	Spencer Bachus	Alabama
Foreign Affairs	Ileana Ros Lehtinen	Florida
Homeland Security	Peter King	New York
Judiciary	Lamar Smith	Texas
Natural Resources	Doc Hastings	Washington
Oversight and Government Reform	Darrell Issa	California
Rules	David Dreier	California
Science, Space and Technology	Ralph Hall	Texas
Small Business	Sam Graves	Missouri
Transportation and Infrastructure	John Mica	Florida
Veterans' Affairs	Jeff Miller	Florida
Ways and Means	Dave Camp	Michigan

Judicial branch

		President who appointed	Year
Chief Justice	John Roberts	George W. Bush	2005
Associate Justices	Antonin Scalia	Ronald Reagan	1986
	Anthony Kennedy	Ronald Reagan	1988
	Clarence Thomas	George H. W. Bush	1991
	Ruth Bader Ginsburg	Bill Clinton	1993
	Stephen Breyer	Bill Clinton	1994
	Samuel Alito	George W. Bush	2006
	Sonia Sotomayor	Barack Obama	2009
	Elena Kagan	Barack Obama	2010